Seamless
CROCHET

TECHNIQUES AND MOTIFS FOR
JOIN-AS-YOU-GO DESIGNS

KRISTIN OMDAHL

INTERWEAVE
interweave.com

EDITOR **KATRINA LOVING**
TECHNICAL EDITOR **KAREN MANTHEY**
DIAGRAMS **KAREN MANTHEY**
DESIGNER **KARLA BAKER**
PHOTOGRAPHER **JOE HANCOCK**
ILLUSTRATOR **ANN SABIN SWANSON**
PRODUCTION **KATHERINE JACKSON**

Interweave Press LLC
201 East Fourth Street
Loveland, CO 80537
interweave.com

Printed in China by Asia Pacific Offset Ltd.

Library of Congress
Cataloging-in-Publication Data

Omdahl, Kristin.

Seamless crochet : techniques and designs for
join-as-you-go motifs /
Kristin Omdahl.

   p. cm.

ISBN 978-1-59668-297-9

1. Crocheting--Patterns. I. Title.

TT825.O4395 2011

746.43'4--dc23

2011019663

10 9 8 7 6 5 4 3 2 1

dedication

*To Marlon, my Shark Hunter and French photographer
extraordinaire. You inspire me always. I love you infinitely.*

acknowledgments

Thank you to my friends and family for your patience and
understanding when I disappear for a book deadline. Thank you
to the incredibly talented staff of Interweave, especially Annie
Bakken, Rebecca Campbell, Jaime Guthals, Katrina Loving,
Elisabeth Malzahn, and Marilyn Murphy: I appreciate your
kindness, support, and talents very much and am grateful for
all you do. Thank you to Cathy Dipierro and Karen Manthey for
their special technical skills. Thank you to Joe Hancock, Jessica
Shinyeda, and Kathy MacKay for making these pages so beautiful!

contents

introduction

It is with great enthusiasm that I present this book to you. When I first discovered the technique of creating and joining motifs without the need for cutting the yarn between them, I wanted to squeal with delight. Over the last couple of years, I have been exploring the technique and coming up with new motifs to showcase fun crochet projects with a minimum of tails to weave in (often only two!). Imagine the possibilities that this technique can create. There are so many wonderful things to make with motifs, especially when you don't have to spend the extra time weaving in all those yarn tails!

Each project in this book is preceded by the motif used in it. I kept the projects fairly simple in order to allow you to become comfortable with the technique. There are many one-skein projects, and many of the motifs are only one or two rounds. However, I've also included some projects that will allow you to take this technique to the next level by exploring how to manipulate motifs for shaping. With a focus on gifts (perfect for friends and family or for a gift to yourself), the collection of patterns in this book will bring you and yours so much happiness. From hats and scarves to baby blankets, home décor items, and shawls, there is something for everyone!

I thoroughly enjoyed this process of exploring the seamless, tail-free construction of crochet motifs. My hope is that, through this book and accompanying DVD, you will enjoy it as much as I did. Learning a new technique is a process, requiring patience and a learning curve. Always remember to breathe, relax, and most importantly—have fun with crochet! This technique requires looking at crochet motifs from a totally different perspective, though I am not suggesting that you abandon everything you know about traditional crochet motifs. On the contrary! This is simply a new, unusual, and vastly useful technique to add to your crochet repertoire.

shawls

I love the geometric texture of crochet motif fabric, but I used to shy away from motif-based shawls because of all the ends to weave in. I was also wary because you usually see both sides of the fabric on a shawl, and I often worried about ends sneaking back out and showing after some wear. In this collection of seamless motif shawls, I used a variety of construction techniques to show how many different ways you can use this technique to eliminate worries about multiple tails that can pop back out. Try swapping the different motifs and construction methods featured here for use in a wide variety of other projects.

blue lagoon
SWIRLING HEXAGON SHAWL

There's no denying that I love the twisting turns of a spiral, a motif that is often displayed in my designs. So, imagine my delight with this particular hexagon-shaped spiral motif, which also fits together as a circular-motif fabric of twisty-petal flowers! This motif is worked in double crochet and chains, and the edges of adjacent motifs are joined with simple slip stitches for a smooth fabric. The result is a visually stunning shawl that will be a striking addition to any ensemble.

YARN

Chunky weight (#5 Bulky).

shown: Malabrigo Yarn, Rios (100% superwash Merino wool; 210 yd [192 m]/3.5 oz [100 g]): 4 skeins of #855 aguas.

HOOK

I/9 (5.5 mm) or size needed to obtain gauge.

NOTIONS

Tapestry needle for weaving in ends.

GAUGE

1 motif = 6½" (16.5 cm) in diameter after blocking.

FINISHED SIZE

52" wide x 29" deep (132 x 73.5 cm).

blue lagoon *motif*

STITCH DIAGRAM A

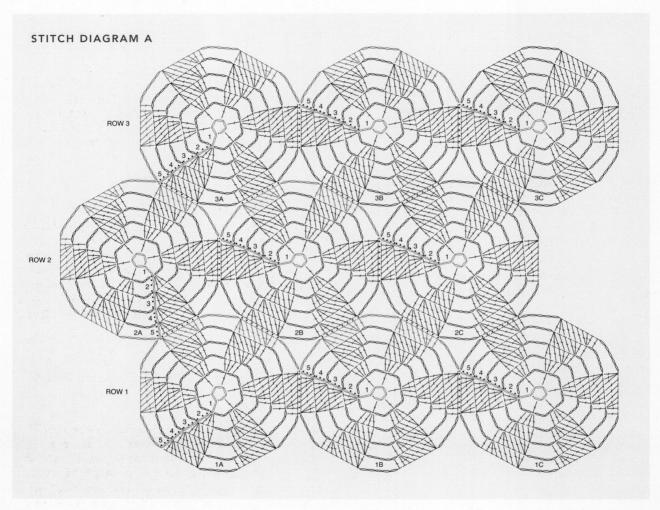

Refer to Stitch Diagram A above for assistance.

Motif 1A

RND 1: Ch 5 + (3 x 5) = 20, sl st in 5th ch from hook to form ring, sl st in ea of next 3 chs (counts as dc), [ch 4, dc in ring] 5 times, ch 4, sl st in top of beg ch-3.

RND 2: Sl st in ea of next 3 chs (counts as dc), 3 dc in next st (top of ch-3 in prev rnd here and throughout), [ch 4, dc in next ch-4 sp, 3 dc in next st] 5 times, ch 4, sl st in top of beg ch-3.

RND 3: Sl st in ea of next 3 chs (counts as dc), 3 dc in next st, dc in next st, dc2tog over next 2 sts, [ch 4, dc in next ch-4 sp, 3 dc in next st, dc in next st, dc2tog over next 2 sts] 5 times, ch 4, sl st to top of beg ch-3.

RND 4: Sl st in ea of next 3 chs (counts as dc), 3 dc in next st, dc in ea of next 2 sts, dc3tog over next 3 sts, [ch 5, dc in next ch-4 sp, 3 dc in next st, dc in ea of next 2 sts, dc3tog over next 3 sts] 5 times, ch 5, sl st to top of beg ch-3.

RND 5: Sl st in ea of next 3 beg chs (counts as dc), 3 dc in next st, dc in ea of next 3 sts, dc3tog over next 3 sts, [ch 5, dc in next ch-5 sp, 3 dc in next st, dc in ea of next 3 sts, dc3tog over next 3 sts] twice.

Motif 1B

Rep Rnds 1–4 of Motif 1A.

RND 5: Sl st in ea of next 3 beg chs (counts as beg dc), sl st in dc on adjacent motif, [dc in next st, sl st in dc on adjacent motif] 3 times in same st, [dc in next st, sl st in dc on adjacent motif] 3 times, dc3tog over next 3 sts, sl st in dc on adjacent motif, [ch 5, dc in next ch-5 sp, 3 dc in next st, dc in ea of next 3 sts, dc3tog over next 3 sts] 3 times.

Motif 1C

Rep Rnds 1–4 of Motif 1A.

RND 5: Sl st in ea of next 3 beg ch (counts as beg dc), sl st in dc on adjacent motif, [dc in next st, sl st in dc on adjacent motif] 3 times in same st, [dc in next st, sl st in dc on adjacent motif] 3 times, dc3tog over next 3 sts, sl st in dc on adjacent motif, ch 5, [dc in next ch-5 sp, 3 dc in next st, dc in ea of next 3 sts, dc3tog over next 3 sts, ch 5] 5 times.

Working across incomplete motifs in row 1, *sl st in sp bet motifs (around sl st), [ch 5, dc in next ch-5 sp, 3 dc in next st, dc in ea of next 3 sts, dc3tog over next 3 sts] twice*, ch 5. Rep from * to * once.

Motif 2A

Rep Rnds 1–4 of Motif 1A.

RND 5: Sl st in ea of next 3 beg chs (counts as beg dc), sl st in dc on adjacent motif, [dc in next st, sl st in dc on adjacent motif] 3 times in same st, [dc in next st, sl st in dc on adjacent motif] 3 times, dc3tog over next 3 sts, sl st in dc on adjacent motif, ch 5, dc in next ch-5 sp, 3 dc in next st, dc in ea of next 3 sts, dc3tog over next 3 sts.

Motif 2B

Rep Rnds 1–4 of Motif 1A.

RND 5: Sl st in ea of next 3 beg chs (counts as beg dc),sl st in dc on adjacent motif, *[dc in next st, sl st in dc on adjacent motif] 3 times in same st, [dc in next st, sl st in dc on adjacent motif] 3 times, dc3tog over next 3 sts, sl st in dc on adjacent motif, ch 5**, dc in next ch-5 sp, sl st in dc on adjacent square. Rep from * once. Rep from * to ** once, dc in next ch-5 sp, 3 dc in next st, dc in ea of next 3 sts, dc3tog over next 3 sts.

Motif 2C

Rep Rnds 1–4 of Motif 1A.

RND 5: Sl st in ea of next 3 beg chs (counts as beg dc), sl st in dc on adjacent motif, *[dc in next st, sl st in dc on adja-cent motif] 3 times in same st, [dc in next st, sl st in dc on adjacent motif] 3 times, dc3tog over next 3 sts, sl st in dc on adjacent motif, ch 5**, dc in next ch-5 sp, sl st in dc on adjacent square. Rep from * once. Rep from * to ** once, [dc in next ch-5 sp, 3 dc in next st, dc in ea of next 3 sts, dc3tog over next 3 sts, ch 5] 3 times.

Working across incomplete motifs in row 2, sl st in sp bet motifs (around sl st), [ch 5, dc in next ch-5 sp, 3 dc in next st, dc in ea of next 3 sts, dc3tog over next 3 sts] twice, ch 5, sl st in sp bet motifs (around sl st), ch 5, dc in next ch-5 sp, 3 dc in next st, dc in ea of next 3 sts, dc3tog over next 3 sts.

Motif 3A

Rep Rnds 1–4 of Motif 1A.

RND 5: Sl st in ea of next 3 beg chs (counts as beg dc), sl st in dc on adjacent motif, *[dc in next st, sl st in dc on adjacent motif] 3 times in same st, [dc in next st, sl st in dc on adjacent motif] 3 times, dc3tog over next 3 sts, sl st in dc on adjacent motif, ch 5*, dc in next ch-5 sp, sl st in dc on adjacent square. Rep from * to * once, dc in next ch-5 sp, 3 dc in next st, dc in ea of next 3 sts, dc3tog over next 3 sts.

Motif 3B

Rep Motif 2B.

Motif 3C

Rep Rnds 1–4 of Motif 1A.

RND 5: Sl st in ea of next 3 beg chs (counts as beg dc), sl st in dc on adjacent motif, *[dc in next st, sl st in dc on adjacent motif] 3 times in same st, [dc in next st, sl st in dc on adjacent motif] 3 times, dc3tog over next 3 sts, sl st in dc on adjacent motif, ch 5*, dc in next ch-5 sp, sl st in dc on adjacent square. Rep from * to * once, [dc in next ch-5 sp, 3 dc in next st, dc in ea of next 3 sts, dc3tog over next 3 sts, ch 5] 4 times.

Working across incomplete motifs in row 3, sl st in sp bet motifs (around sl st), [ch 5, dc in next ch-5 sp, 3 dc in next st, dc in ea of next 3 sts, dc3tog over next 3 sts] twice, ch 5, sl st in sp bet motifs (around sl st), [ch 5, dc in next ch-5 sp, 3 dc in next st, dc in ea of next 3 sts, dc3tog over next 3 sts] 3 times, ch 5.

Working along incomplete motifs in column A, sl st in sp bet motifs (around sl st), [ch 5, dc in ch-5 sp, 3 dc in next st, dc in ea of next 3 sts, dc3tog] 3 times, ch 5, sl st in sp bet motifs (around sl st), ch 5, work dc in next ch-5 sp, 3 dc in next st, dc in ea of next 3 sts, dc3tog over next 3 sts, ch 5, sl st to first ch at beg ch on Motif 1A. Fasten off.

Blue Lagoon Swirling Hexagon Shawl

Refer to the instructions for the Blue Lagoon Swirling Hexagon Motif on page 10 for motifs referenced in these instructions; refer to Stitch Diagram B at right and the Construction Diagram on page 14 for assistance.

Motif 1

Work same as Motif 1A.

Motifs 2–3

Work same as Motif 1B.

Motif 4

Work same as Motif 1C

Working across incomplete motifs in row 1, *sl st in sp bet motifs (around sl st), [ch 5, dc in next ch-5 sp, 3 dc in next st, dc in ea of next 3 sts, dc3tog over next 3 sts] twice**, ch 5. Rep from * twice. Rep from * to ** once.

Motif 5

Work same as Motif 2A.

Motifs 6–8

Work same as Motif 2B.

Motif 9

Rep Rnds 1–4 of Motif 1A.

RND 5: Sl st in ea of next 3 beg chs (counts as beg dc), sl st in dc on adjacent motif, *[dc in next st, sl st in dc on adjacent motif] 3 times in same st, [dc in next st, sl st in dc on adjacent motif] 3 times, dc3tog over next 3 sts, sl st in dc on adjacent motif, ch 5*, dc in next ch-5 sp, sl st in dc on adjacent square. Rep from * to * once, [dc in next ch-5 sp, 3 dc in next st, dc in ea of next 3 sts, dc3tog over next 3 sts, ch 5] 4 times.

Working across incomplete motifs in row 2, *sl st in sp bet motifs (around sl st), [ch 5, dc in next ch-5 sp, 3 dc in next st, dc in ea of next 3 sts, dc3tog over next 3 sts] twice, ch 5. Rep from * 3 times. Sl st in sp bet motifs (around sl st), [ch 5, dc in next ch-5 sp, 3 dc in next st, dc in ea of next 3 sts, dc3tog over next 3 sts] twice.

Motif 10

Work same as Motif 2A.

Motifs 11–14

Work same as Motif 2B.

Motif 15

Rep Motif 9.

Working across incomplete motifs in row 3, *sl st in sp bet motifs (around sl st), [ch 5, dc in next ch-5 sp, 3 dc in next st, dc in ea of next 3 sts, dc3tog over next 3 sts] twice, ch 5. Rep from * 4 times. Sl st in sp bet motifs (around sl st), [ch 5, dc in next ch-5 sp, 3 dc in next st, dc in ea of next 3 sts, dc3tog over next 3 sts] twice.

Motif 16

Work same as Motif 2A.

Motifs 17–21

Work same as Motif 2B.

Motif 22

Rep Motif 9.

Working across incomplete motifs in row 4, *sl st in sp bet motifs (around sl st), [ch 5, dc in next ch-5 sp, 3 dc in next st, dc in ea of next 3 sts, dc3tog over next 3 sts] twice, ch 5. Rep from * 5 times. Sl st in sp bet motifs (around sl st), [ch 5, dc in next ch-5 sp, 3 dc in next st, dc in ea of next 3 sts, dc3tog over next 3 sts] twice.

Note

Shawl is begun from the bottom edge and worked up, starting with 4 motifs on the first row and increasing by 1 motif per row of motifs.

STITCH DIAGRAM B

5 4 3 2 1 · 2 · 3 · 4 · 5
15

5 4 3 2 1
13-14

5 4 3 2 1
12

5 4 3 2 1
11

5 4 3 2 1
9

5 4 3 2 1
7-8

5 4 3 2 1
6

5 4 3 2 1
4

5 4 3 2 1
2-3

1
1 2 3 4 5
ROW 1

1 2 3 4 5
10

ROW 2

ROW 3

Motif 23

Work same as Motif 2A.

Motifs 24–29

Work same as Motif 2B.

Motif 30

Rep Motif 9.

Working across incomplete motifs in row 5, *sl st in sp bet motifs (around sl st), [ch 5, dc in next ch-5 sp, 3 dc in next st, dc in ea of next 3 sts, dc3tog over next 3 sts] twice, ch 5. Rep from * 6 times. Sl st in sp bet motifs (around sl st), [ch 5, dc in next ch-5 sp, 3 dc in next st, dc in ea of next 3 sts, dc3tog over next 3 sts] 4 times, ch 5.

Working along incomplete motifs in column A, *sl st in sp bet motifs (around sl st), [ch 5, dc in ch-5 sp, 3 dc in next st, dc in ea of next 3 sts, dc3tog] twice, ch 5. Rep from * twice. Sl st in sp bet motifs (around sl st), ch 5, dc in next ch-5 sp, 3 dc in next st, dc in ea of next 3 sts, dc3tog over next 3 sts, ch 5, sl st to first ch at beg ch on Motif 1. Fasten off. Weave in ends.

Wet or steam block to finished measurements.

Note: The fiber content (superwash wool) of this yarn is machine washable. If it is easier for you, just wash in the machine, pin and block to finished measurements, and let dry.

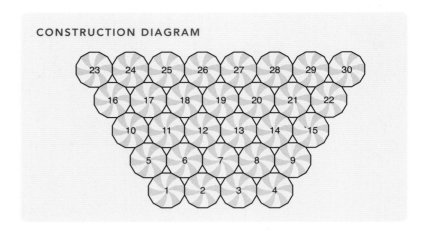

CONSTRUCTION DIAGRAM

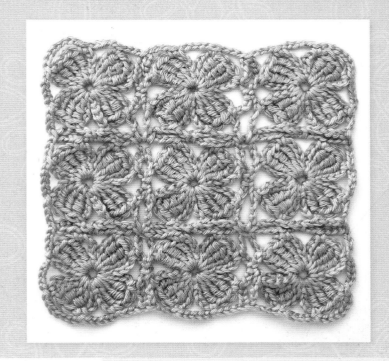

blissful flowers

SHAWL

Worked from the bottom up, a shawl is usually decreased on either side of the center and each side edge, to create a decreasing triangular shape. To achieve this design in motifs that join as you go, we convert the square motif into triangular motifs for the decrease section (thereby reducing additional motif edges for the next row of motifs). The motif is further converted to create a delicate and beautiful flower fringe. Once you are familiar with this technique, wouldn't it make a beautiful raglan pullover?

YARN

DK weight (#3 Light).

shown: Bijou Basin Ranch, Bliss (50% yak/50% Cormo wool; 150 yd [137 m]/2 oz [56 g]): 8 skeins of blush.

HOOK

H/8 (5 mm) or size needed to obtain gauge.

NOTIONS

Tapestry needle to weave in ends.

GAUGE

1 motif = 2½" (6.5 cm) square after blocking.

FINISHED SIZE

68" wide x 28" long (172.7 x 71 cm).

blissful flower *motif*

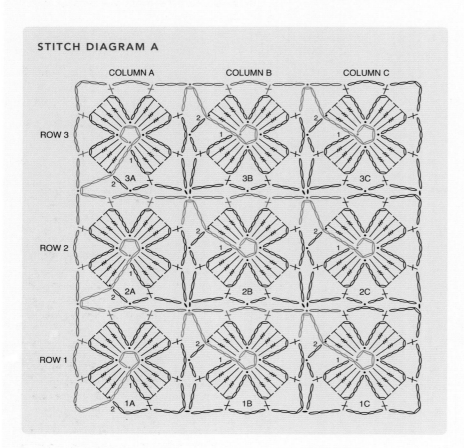

STITCH DIAGRAM A

COLUMN A COLUMN B COLUMN C

ROW 3

3A 3B 3C

ROW 2

2A 2B 2C

ROW 1

1A 1B 1C

Refer to Stitch Diagram A above for assistance.

Motif 1A

RND 1: Ch 5 + 5 + 4 = 14, sl st in 5th ch from hook, [(ch 5, 3 dtr, ch 5, sl st) in ring] 3 times, ch 5, 3 dtr in ring, sl st to 5th ch of beg ch.

RND 2: Ch 5, sc in next ch-5 sp, ch 7, sc in next ch-5 sp, ch 5, sc in next ch-5 sp.

Motif 1B

RND 1: Ch 5 + 5 + 7 = 17, sl st in 5th ch from hook, [(ch 5, 3 dtr, ch 5, sl st) in ring] 3 times, ch 5, 3 dtr in ring, sl st to 5th ch of beg ch.

RND 2: Ch 2, sl st in ch-5 sp on adjacent motif, ch 2, sc in next ch-5 sp on current motif, ch 3, sl st in ch-7 sp on adjacent motif, ch 3, sc in next ch-5 sp on current motif, ch 5, sc in next ch-5 sp, ch 7, sc in next ch-5 sp, ch 5, sc in next ch-5 sp.

Motif 1C

RND 1: Rep Rnd 1 of Motif 1B.

RND 2: Ch 2, sl st in ch-5 sp on adjacent motif, ch 2, sc in next ch-5 sp on current motif, ch 3, sl st in ch-7 sp on adjacent motif, ch 3, sc in next ch-5 sp on current motif, [ch 5, sc in next ch-5 sp, ch 7, sc in next ch-5 sp] twice, ch 5, sc in next ch-5 sp.

Working across incomplete motifs in row 1, ch 3, sl st in 4th ch of ch-7 sp, ch 3, sc in next ch-5 sp, ch 5, sc in next ch-5 sp, ch 3, sl st in 4th ch of ch-7 sp, ch 3, sc in next ch-5 sp, ch 5, sc in next ch-5 sp.

Motif 2A

RND 1: Rep Rnd 1 of Motif 1B.

RND 2: Ch 2, sl st in ch-5 sp on adjacent motif, ch 2, sc in next ch-5 sp on current motif, ch 3, sl st in ch-7 sp on adjacent motif, ch 3, sc in next ch-5 sp on current motif, ch 5, sc in next ch-5 sp.

Motif 2B

RND 1: Rep Rnd 1 of Motif 1B.

RND 2: [Ch 2, sl st in ch-5 sp on adjacent motif, ch 2, sc in next ch-5 sp on current motif, ch 3, sl st in ch-7 sp on adjacent motif, ch 3, sc in next ch-5 sp on current motif] twice, ch 5, sc in next ch-5 sp.

Motif 2C

RND 1: Rep Rnd 1 of Motif 1B.

RND 2: [Ch 2, sl st in ch-5 sp on adjacent motif, ch 2, sc in next ch-5 sp on current motif, ch 3, sl st in ch-7 sp on adjacent motif, ch 3, sc in next ch-5 sp on current motif] twice, ch 5, sc in next ch-5 sp, ch 7, sc in next ch-5 sp, ch 5, sc in next ch-5 sp.

Working across incomplete motifs in Row 2, ch 3, sl st in 4th ch of ch-7 sp, ch 3, sc in next ch-5 sp, ch 5, sc in next ch-5 sp, ch 3, sl st in 4th ch of ch-7 sp, ch 3, sc in next ch-5 sp, ch 5, sc in next ch-5 sp.

Motif 3A

Rep Motif 2A.

Motif 3B

Rep Motif 2B.

Motif 3C

Rep Motif 2C.

Working across incomplete motifs in row 3, ch 3, sl st in 4th ch of ch-7 sp, ch 3, sc in next ch-5 sp, ch 5, sc in next ch-5 sp, ch 3, sl st in 4th ch of ch-7 sp, ch 3, sc in next ch-5 sp, ch 5, sc in next ch-5 sp, ch 7, sc in next ch-5 sp, ch 5, sc in next ch-5 sp.

Working across incomplete motifs in column A, ch 3, sl st in 4th ch of ch-7 sp, ch 3, sc in next ch-5 sp, ch 5, sc in next ch-5 sp, ch 3, sl st in 4th ch of ch-7 sp, ch 3, sc in next ch-5 sp, ch 5, sc in next ch-5 sp, ch 3, sl st to first ch of beg ch to join. Fasten off.

Blissful Flowers Shawl

Refer to Stitch Diagram B on page 21 and the Construction Diagram on page 21 for assistance. Instructions for the Blissful Flower Motif begin on page 18.

Motif 1

RND 1: Ch 5 + 5 + 4 = 14, sl st in 5th ch from hook, [ch 5, 3 dtr, ch 5, sl st in ring] twice, ch 5, 3 dtr in ring, sl st to 5th ch of beg ch-3 petals.

RND 2: Ch 5, sc in next ch-5 sp, ch 7, sc in next ch-5 sp, ch 5, sc in next ch-5 sp,

Motifs 2–15

RND 1: Ch 5 + 5 + 7 = 17, sl st in 5th ch from hook, [ch 5, 3 dtr, ch 5, sl st in ring] 3 times, ch 5, 3 dtr in ring, sl st to 5th ch of beg ch-4 petals.

RND 2: Ch 2, sl st in ch-5 sp on adjacent motif, ch 2, sc in ch-5 sp on current motif, ch 3, sl st in ch-7 sp on adjacent motif, ch 3, sc in next ch-5 sp on current motif, ch 5, sc in next ch-5 sp, ch 7, sc in next ch-5 sp, ch 5, sc in next ch-5 sp.

Motifs 16–17

RND 1: Ch 5 + 5 + 7 = 17, sl st in 5th ch from hook, [ch 5, 3 dtr in ring, ch 5, sl st in ring] twice, ch 5, 3 dtr in ring, sl st to 5th ch of beg ch-3 petals.

RND 2: Ch 2, sl st in ch-5 sp on adjacent motif, ch 2, sc in ch-5 sp on current motif, ch 3, sl st in ch-7 sp on adjacent motif, ch 3, sc in next ch-5 sp on current motif, ch 5, sc in next ch-5 sp, ch 7, sc in next ch-5 sp, ch 5, sc in next ch-5 sp.

Motifs 18–31

Rep Motif 2.

Motif 32

Rep Motif 46.

Working across incomplete Motifs 32–1, ch 3, sl st in 4th ch of ch-7, *ch 3, sc in ch-5 sp on next motif, ch 5, sc in next ch-5 sp, ch 3, sl st in 4th ch of ch-7*. Rep from * to * 13 times, sl st in ea of next 2 ch-7 sps, rep from * to * 14 times.

Motif 33

RND 1: Ch 5 + 5 + 3 = 13, sl st in 5th ch from hook, [ch 5, 3 dtr in ring, ch 5, sl st in ring] twice, ch 5, 3 dtr in ring, sl st to 5th ch of beg ch-3 petals.

RND 2: Ch 2, sl st in ch-5 sp on adjacent motif, ch 2, sc in ch-5 sp on current motif, ch 3, sl st in ch-7 sp on adjacent motif, ch 3, sc in next ch-5 sp on current motif, ch 5, sc in next ch-5 sp.

Motifs 34–45

RND 1: Rep Rnd 1 of Motif 2.

RND 2: [Ch 2, sl st in ch-5 sp on adjacent motif, ch 2, sc in next ch-5 sp on current motif, ch 3, sl st in ch-7 sp on adjacent motif, ch 3, sc in next ch-5 sp on current motif] twice, ch 5, sc in next ch-5 sp.

Motifs 46–47

RND 1: Rep Rnd 1 of Motif 2.

RND 2: [Ch 2, sl st in ch-5 sp on adjacent motif, ch 2, sc in ch-5 sp on current motif, ch 3, sl st in ch-7 sp on adjacent motif, ch 3, sc in next ch-5 sp on current motif] twice, ch 5, sc in next ch-5 sp.

Motifs 48–59

Rep Motif 34.

Motif 60

Rep Motif 46.

Working across incomplete Motifs 60–33, ch 3, sl st in 4th ch of ch-7, *ch 3, sc in ch-5 sp on next motif, ch 5, sc in next ch-5 sp, ch 3, sl st in 4th ch of ch-7*. Rep from * to * 11 times, sl st in ea of next 2 ch-7 sps, rep from * to * 12 times.

Motif 61

Rep Motif 33.

Motifs 62–71

Rep Motif 34.

Motifs 72–73

Rep Motif 46.

CONSTRUCTION DIAGRAM

ROW 1	ROW 2	ROW 3	ROW 4	ROW 5	ROW 6	ROW 7	ROW 8

The construction diagram shows a triangular grid with the following numbered cells:

1, 33, 61, 85, 105, 121, 133, 141, 144, 140, 132, 120, 104, 84, 60, 32
2, 34, 62, 86, 106, 122, 134, 142, 143, 139, 131, 119, 103, 83, 59, 31
3, 35, 63, 87, 107, 123, 135, 138, 130, 118, 102, 82, 58, 30
4, 36, 64, 88, 108, 124, 136, 137, 129, 117, 101, 81, 57, 29
5, 37, 65, 89, 109, 125, 128, 116, 100, 80, 56, 28
6, 38, 66, 90, 110, 126, 127, 115, 99, 79, 55, 27
7, 39, 67, 91, 111, 114, 98, 78, 54, 26
8, 40, 68, 92, 112, 113, 97, 77, 53, 25
9, 41, 69, 93, 96, 76, 52, 24
10, 42, 70, 94, 95, 75, 51, 23
11, 43, 71, 74, 50, 22
12, 44, 72, 73, 49, 21
13, 45, 48, 20
14, 46, 47, 19
15, 18
16, 17

STITCH DIAGRAM B

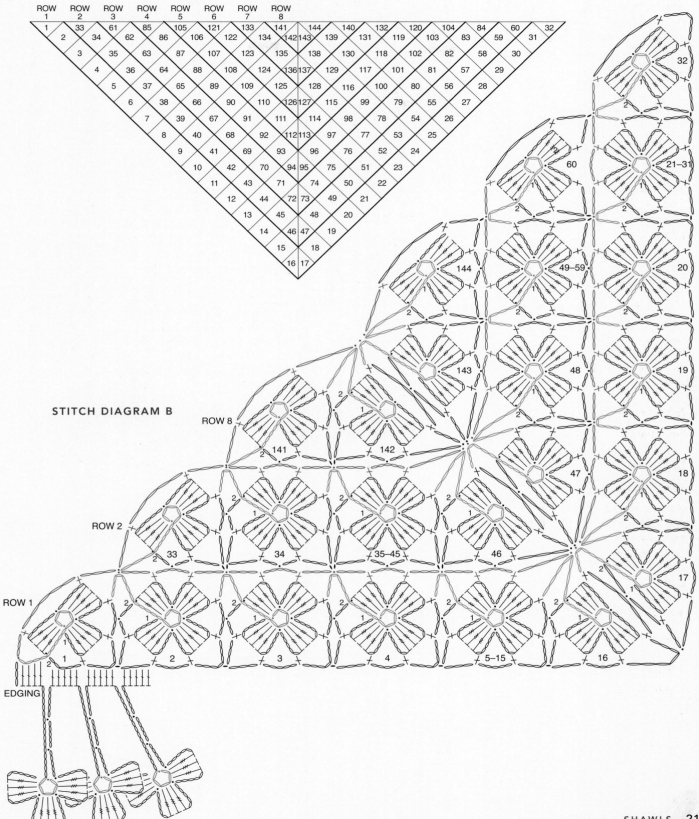

ROW 8

ROW 2

ROW 1

EDGING

Labels within diagram: 141, 142, 33, 34, 35–45, 46, 1, 2, 3, 4, 5–15, 16, 17, 18, 19, 20, 21–31, 32, 47, 48, 49–59, 60, 143, 144

Motifs 74–83

Rep Motif 34.

Motif 84

Rep Motif 46.

Working across incomplete Motifs 84–61, ch 3, sl st in 4th ch of ch-7, *ch 3, sc in ch-5 sp on next motif, ch 5, sc in next ch-5 sp, ch 3, sl st in 4th ch of ch-7*. Rep from * to * 9 times, sl st in ea of next 2 ch-7 sps, rep from * to * 10 times.

Motif 85

Rep Motif 33.

Motifs 86–93

Rep Motif 34.

Motifs 94–95

Rep Motif 46.

Motifs 96–103

Rep Motif 34.

Motif 104

Rep Motif 46.

Working across incomplete Motifs 104–85, ch 3, sl st in 4th ch of ch-7, *ch 3, sc in ch-5 sp on next motif, ch 5, sc in next ch-5 sp, ch 3, sl st in 4th ch of ch-7*. Rep from * to * 7 times, sl st in ea of next 2 ch-7 sps, rep from * to * 8 times.

Motif 105

Rep Motif 33.

Motifs 106–111

Rep Motif 34.

Motifs 112–113

Rep Motif 46.

Motifs 114–119

Rep Motif 34.

Motif 120

Rep Motif 46.

Working across incomplete Motifs 120–105, ch

3, sl st in 4th ch of ch-7, *ch 3, sc in ch-5 sp on next motif, ch 5, sc in next ch-5 sp, ch 3, sl st in 4th ch of ch-7*. Rep from * to * 5 times, sl st in ea of next 2 ch-7 sps, rep from * to * 6 times.

Motif 121

Rep Motif 33.

Motifs 122–125

Rep Motif 34.

Motifs 126–127

Rep Motif 46.

Motifs 128–131

Rep Motif 34.

Motif 132

Rep Motif 46.

Working across incomplete Motifs 132–121, ch 3, sl st in 4th ch of ch-7, *ch 3, sc in ch-5 sp on next motif, ch 5, sc in next ch-5 sp, ch 3, sl st in 4th ch of ch-7*. Rep from * to * 3 times, sl st in ea of next 2 ch-7 sps, rep from * to * 4 times.

Motif 133

Rep Motif 33.

Motifs 134–135

Rep Motif 34.

Motifs 136–137

Rep Motif 46.

Motifs 138–139

Rep Motif 34.

Motif 140

Rep Motif 46.

Working across incomplete Motifs 140–133, ch 3, sl st in 4th ch of ch-7, *ch 3, sc in ch-5 sp on next motif, ch 5, sc in next ch-5 sp, ch 3, sl st in 4th ch of ch-7*. Rep from * to * once, sl st in ea of next 2 ch-7 sps, rep from * to * twice.

Motif 141

Rep Motif 33.

Motif 142–144

Rep Motif 46.

Working across incomplete Motifs 144–141, ch 3, [sl st in 4th ch of ch-7] 3 times, ch 3, sc in ch-5 sp on next motif, ch 5, sc in next ch-5 sp.

Working across side of incomplete Motifs 133, 121, 105, 85, 61, 33, and 1, [ch 3, sl st in 4th of ch-7, ch 3, sc in next ch-5 sp on next motif, ch 5, sc in next ch-5 sp] 7 times, ch 3, sl st to first ch of beg ch to join (counts as ch-7 sp). Do not fasten off.

Edging

Working across bottom edges of shawl, ch 3, work 4 dc in same ch-sp, *ch 20, sl st in 5th ch from hook to form ring, [ch 5, 3 dtr in ring, ch 5, sl st in ring] 3 times, [ch 5, skip next 4 chs, sl st in next ch] twice, ch 5, 5 dc in next ch-sp on shawl edge. Rep from * across entire lower "V" edge of shawl to corner ch-7 sp of Motif 32. Fasten off. Weave in ends.

Wet block, pin to finished measurements, and let dry.

eden tile
RECTANGULAR WRAP

The smallest and simplest of square motifs make a beautiful textured fabric, but who wants to weave in hundreds of loose ends? This one-round join-as-you-go square motif is quick to memorize, making this wrap a relaxing project. The edging is worked in another crochet technique called Bruges Lace that is joined to the edge of the shawl with chains. Drape this wrap around your shoulders for extra warmth or use it as a chunky scarf.

YARN

DK weight (#3 Light).

shown: Lorna's Laces, Honor (70% baby alpaca, 30% silk; 275 yd [251.5 m]/3.5 oz [100 g]): 5 skeins of turtle rodeo (multicolor featuring greens, browns, and orange).

HOOK

H/8 (5 mm) or size needed to obtain gauge.

NOTIONS

Tapestry needle for weaving in ends and sewing.

GAUGE

1 square tile = 2" (5 cm) square after blocking.

FINISHED SIZE

80" wide x 24" long (203.5 x 61 cm).
Wrap fabric is 36 squares wide x 11 squares long.

eden tile *motif*

STITCH DIAGRAM A

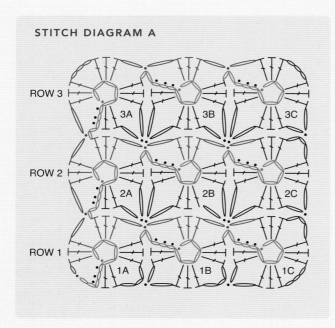

STITCH DIAGRAM A

ROW 3

3A   3B   3C

ROW 2

2A   2B   2C

ROW 1

1A   1B   1C

Refer to Stitch Diagram A above for assistance.

Motif 1A

RND 1: Ch 5 + 3 + 3 = 11, sl st in 5th ch from hook to form ring. Sl st in ea of next 3 chs (counts as dc), 2 dc in ring, ch 3, 3 dc in ring.

Motif 1B

Rnd 1: Ch 5 + 3 + 3 = 11, sl st in 5th ch from hook to form ring. Sl st in ea of next 3 chs (counts as dc), 2 dc in ring, ch 1, sl st in corner sp on adjacent motif, ch 1, 3 dc in ring.

Motif 1C

RND 1: Ch 5 + 3 + 3 = 11, sl st in 5th ch from hook to form ring. Sl st in ea of next 3 chs (counts as dc), 2 dc in ring, ch 1, sl st in corner sp on adjacent motif, ch 1, (3 dc, ch 3, 3 dc) in ring.

Working across incomplete motifs in row 1, *ch 1, sl st in 2nd ch of ch-3 sp, ch 1, 3 dc in next motif's ring. Rep from * once.

Motif 2A

Ch 11, sl st in 5th ch from hook to form ring. Sl st in ea of next 3 chs (counts as dc), 2 dc in ring, ch 1, sl st in corner sp on adjacent motif, ch 1, 3 dc in same ring.

Motif 2B

Ch 11, sl st in 5th ch from hook to form ring. Sl st in ea of next 3 chs (counts as dc), 2 dc in ring, [ch 1, sl st in corner sp on adjacent motif, ch 1, 3 dc in same ring] twice.

Motif 2C

Ch 11, sl st in 5th ch from hook to form ring. Sl st in ea of next 3 chs (counts as dc), 2 dc in ring, [ch 1, sl st in corner sp on adjacent motif, ch 1, 3 dc in same ring] twice, ch 3, 3 dc in same ring.

Working across incomplete motifs in row 2, *ch 1, sl st in 2nd ch of ch-3 sp, ch 1, 3 dc in next ring. Rep from * once.

Motif 3A

Rep Motif 2A.

Motif 3B

Rep Motif 2B.

Motif 3C

Rep Motif 2C.

Working across incomplete motifs in row 3, *ch 1, sl st in 2nd ch of ch-2, ch 1, 3 dc in next motif's ring. Rep from * once, ch 3, 3 dc in same ring.

Working across side edge of incomplete motifs in column A, *ch 1, sl st in 2nd ch of ch-3 sp, ch 1, 3 dc in next motif's ring. Rep from * once, ch 1, sl st in top of ch-3 at beg to join. Fasten off.

Tiled Rectangular Wrap

Refer to the instructions for the Tile Motif at left; refer to Stitch Diagram B on page 28 for assistance.

Motif 1

RND 1: Ch 5 + 3 + 3 = 11, sl st in 5th ch from hook to form ring. Sl st in ea of next 3 chs (counts as dc), 2 dc in ring, ch 3, 3 dc in ring.

Motifs 2–35

RND 1: Ch 5 + 3 + 3 = 11, sl st in 5th ch from hook to form ring. Sl st in ea of next 3 chs (counts as dc), 2 dc in ring, ch 1, sl st in corner sp on adjacent motif, ch 1, 3 dc in ring.

Motif 36

RND 1: Ch 5 + 3 + 3 = 11, sl st in 5th ch from hook to form ring. Sl st in ea of next 3 chs (counts as dc), 2 dc in ring, ch 1, sl st in corner sp on adjacent motif, ch 1, (3 dc, ch 3, 3 dc) in ring.

Working across incomplete motifs in row 1, *ch 1, sl st in 2nd ch of ch-3 sp, ch 1, 3 dc in next ring. Rep from * across.

Motif 37

Ch 11, sl st in 5th ch from hook to form ring, sl st in each of next 3 chs (counts as dc), 2 dc in ring, ch 1, sl st in corner sp on adjacent motif, ch 1, work 3 dc in same ring.

Motifs 38–71

Ch 11, sl st in 5th ch from hook to form ring, sl st in each of next 3 chs (counts as dc), 2 dc in ring, [ch 1, sl st in ch-3 sp on adjacent motif, ch 1, 3 dc in same ring] twice.

Motif 72

Ch 11, sl st in 5th ch from hook to form ring, sl st in each of next 3 chs (counts as dc), 2 dc in ring, [ch 1, sl st in corner sp on adjacent motif, ch 1, 3 dc in same ring] twice, ch 3, 3 dc in same ring.

Working across incomplete motifs in row 2, *ch 1, sl st in 2nd ch of ch-3 sp, ch 1, 3 dc in next ring. Rep from * across.

STITCH DIAGRAM B

Motifs 73–396

Rep Motifs 37–72 nine times , including Completion Rows.

Working across side edge of incomplete motifs 361, 325, 289, 253, 217, 181, 145, 109, 73, 37, and 1, ch 3, 3 dc in same ring, *ch 1, sl st in 2nd ch of ch-3 sp ch 1, 3 dc in next motif's ring. Rep from * across to Motif 1, sl st in top of ch-3 at beg to join. Do not fasten off.

Bruges Lace Edging

ROW 1: Ch 14, turn, dc in 8th ch from hook, dc in each of next 3 chs, turn.

ROW 2: Ch 3, sl st in 2nd of 3 dc on adjacent motif, ch 3, turn, 1 dc in each of next 4 dc, turn.

ROW 3: Ch 7, turn, dc in each of next 4 dc.

ROW 4: Ch 3, sl st in next corner join on adjacent motif, ch 3, turn, 1 dc in ea of next 4 dc, turn.

ROW 5: Ch 7, turn, dc in ea of next 4 dc.

ROWS 67–145: Rep Rows 2–5 across long edge of wrap.

ROWS 146–161: Ch 7, turn, dc in ea of next 4 dc.

ROW 162: Ch 3, insert hook in ea of last 3 ch-7 loops made, work a sl st, ch 3, turn, dc in ea of next 4 dc.

ROW 163: Ch 7, turn, dc in ea of next 4 dc.

ROW 164: Ch 3, sl st in next corresponding ch-7 loop, ch 3, turn, dc in ea of next 4 dc, turn.

ROWS 165–173: Rep Rows 163–164 four times, then rep Row 163.

ROW 174: Ch 3, sl st in next corner join on adjacent motif, ch 3, turn, dc in ea of next 4 dc, turn.

ROW 175: Ch 7, turn, dc in ea of next 4 dc.

ROW 176: Ch 3, sl st in next corner join on adjacent motif, ch 3, turn, dc in ea of next 4 dc, turn.

ROW 177: Ch 3, sl st in last 2 ch-7 loops made, ch 3, turn, dc in ea of next 4 dc.

ROWS 178–188: Rep Rows 163–164 five times, then rep 163.

ROWS 189–205: Rep Rows 157–173.

ROW 206: Ch 3, sk next square on wrap, sl st in 2nd dc of 3-dc group on adjacent motif, ch 3, turn, dc in ea of next 4 dc.

ROWS 207–208: Ch 7, turn, dc in ea of next 4 dc.

ROW 209: Ch 3, sl st in last 3 ch-7 loops made, ch 3, turn, dc in ea of next 4 dc.

ROWS 210–359: Rep Row 180–209 five times.

ROW 360–385: Rep Rows 180–205.

ROW 386: Ch 3, sl st in next corner join on adjacent motif, ch 3, turn, dc in ea of next 4 dc, turn.

ROW 387: Ch 7, turn, dc in ea of next 4 dc.

ROWS 388–459: Rep Rows 386–387 thirty-six times.

ROWS 460–700: Rep Rows 146–386. Fasten off, leaving a sewing length. Sew last row to first row, across 4 dc and corresponding chs.

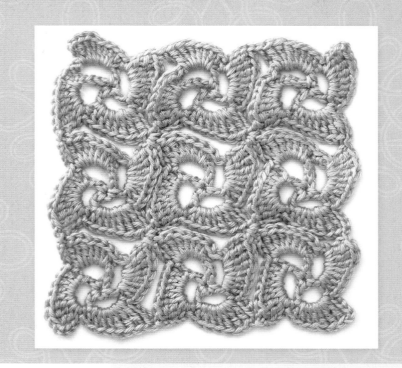

ninja star
SHAWLETTE

The subtle spiral and the shape of this motif remind me of ninja stars (also known as throwing stars): hence the name. When crocheted in the gorgeous silk yarn featured here, the motif is so pretty and feminine it creates an enchanting shawl. It is crocheted from the top down, adding more motifs to create the increases necessary for the growing triangular shape. The fringe is a special edging stitch that reminds me of chandelier earrings. This shawl would look so lovely dangling over bare shoulders at a formal event.

YARN

DK weight (#3 Light).

shown: Tilli Tomas, Plie (100% silk; 125 yd [114.5 m]/1.75 oz [50 g]): 3 balls of eternal diva (medium blue).

HOOK

F/5 (3.75 mm) or size needed to obtain gauge.

NOTIONS

Tapestry needle for weaving in ends.

GAUGE

1 motif = 3" (7.5 cm) square after blocking.

FINISHED SIZE

58" wide x 29" long (147.5 x 73.5 cm) including edging.

ninja star *motif*

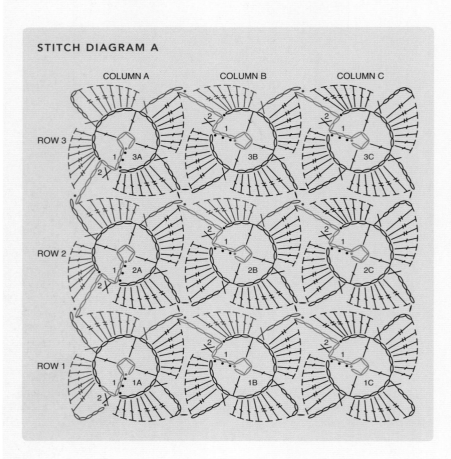

STITCH DIAGRAM A

Refer to Stitch Diagram A above for assistance.

Motif 1A

RND 1: Ch 4 + 3 + 2 = 9, sl st in 4th ch from hook to form ring, sl st in ea of next 3 chs (counts as dc), *ch 5, dc in ring. Rep from * twice, ch 3, sl st in first ch of beg ch (counts as ch-5).

RND 2: Sc in same ch-2 sp, (4 dc, 3 tr, ch 5, sc) in next ch-5 sp, (4 dc, 3 tr) in next ch-5 sp.

Motif 1B

RND 1: Ch 4 + 3 + 2 + 5 = 14, sl st in 4th ch from hook to form ring, sl st in ea of next 3 chs (counts as dc), *ch 5, dc in ring. Rep from * twice, ch 3, sl st in 6th ch of beg ch (counts as ch-5 sp).

RND 2: Sc in same ch-2 sp, (4 dc, 3 tr) in next ch-5 sp, sl st in adjacent motif's ch-5 sp, ch 4, sc in same ch-5 sp on current motif. (4 dc, 3 tr, ch 5, sc) in next ch-5 sp, (4 dc, 3 tr) in next ch-5 sp.

Motif 1C

RND 1: Rep Rnd 1 of Motif 1B.

RND 2: Sc in same ch-2 sp, (4 dc, 3 tr) in next ch-5 sp, sl st in adjacent motif's ch-5 sp, ch 4, sc in same ch-5 sp on current motif. *(4 dc, 3 tr, ch 5, sc) in next ch-5 sp. Rep from * once, (4 dc, 3 tr) in next ch-5 sp.

Working across incomplete motifs in row 1, [sl st in first ch of beg ch, ch 4, sc in next ch-5 sp, (4 dc, 3 tr) in next ch-5 sp] twice.

Motif 2A

RND 1: Rep Rnd 1 of Motif 1B.

RND 2: Sc in same ch-2 sp, (4 dc, 3 tr) in next ch-5 sp, sl st in adjacent motif's ch-4 sp, ch 4, sc in same ch-5 sp on current motif. (4 dc, 3 tr) in next ch-5 sp.

Motif 2B

RND 1: Rep Rnd 1 of Motif 1B.

RND 2: Sc in same ch-2 sp, *(4 dc, 3 tr) in next ch-5 sp, sl st in adjacent motif's ch-4 sp, ch 4, sc in same ch-5 sp on current motif. Rep from * once. (4 dc, 3 tr) in next ch-5 sp.

Motif 2C

RND 1: Rep Rnd 1 of Motif 1B.

RND 2: Sc in same ch-2 sp,*(4 dc, 3 tr) in next ch-5 sp, sl st in adjacent motif's ch-4 sp, ch 4, sc in same ch-5 sp on current motif. Rep from * once, (4 dc, 3 tr, ch 5, sc) in next ch-5 sp, (4 dc, 3 tr) in next ch-5 sp.

Working across incomplete motifs in row 2, [sl st in first ch of beg ch, ch 4, sc in next ch-5 sp, (4 dc, 3 tr) in next ch-5 sp] twice.

Motif 3A

Rep Motif 2A.

Motif 3B

Rep Motif 2B.

Motif 3C

Rep Motif 2C.

Working across incomplete motifs in row 3, [sl st in first ch of beg ch, ch 4, sc in next ch-5 sp, (4 dc, 3 tr) in next ch-5 sp] twice.

Working across side edge of incomplete motifs in column A, ch 5, sc in same ch-5 sp, (4 dc, 3 tr) in next ch-5 sp, [sl st in first ch of beg ch, ch 4, sc in next ch-5 sp, (4 dc, 3 tr) in next ch-5 sp] twice, ch 5, sl st to first sc at beg of Row 2 of Motif 1A. Fasten off.

Ninja Stars Shawlette

Refer to Stitch Diagram B and the Construction Diagram on page 37 for assistance. Instructions for the Ninja Star Motif begin at left.

Motif 1

RND 1: Ch 4 + 3 + 2 = 9, sl st in 4th ch from hook to make ring, sl st in ea of next 3 chs (counts as dc), *ch 5, dc in ring. Rep from * twice, ch 3, sl st in 2nd ch of beg ch (counts as ch 5).

RND 2: Sc in same ch-2 sp, (4 dc, 3 tr, ch 5, sc) in next ch-5 sp, (4 dc, 3 tr) in next ch-5 sp.

Motif 2

RND 1: Ch 4 + 3 + 2 + 5 = 14, sl st in 4th ch from hook to make ring, sl st in ea of next 3 chs (counts as dc), *ch 5, dc in ring. Rep from * twice, ch 3, sl st in 6th ch of beg ch (counts as ch-5 sp).

RND 2: Sc in same ch-5 sp, (4 dc, 3 tr) in next ch-5 sp, sl st in adjacent ch-5 sp on Motif 1, ch 4, sc in same ch-5 sp on current motif. *(4 dc, 3 tr, ch 5, sc) in next ch-5 sp. Rep from * once, (4 dc, 3 tr) in next ch-5 sp, sl st to first ch of beg ch.

Cont as follows to complete more of Rnd 2 of Motif 1, ch 4, sc in ch-5 sp, (4 dc, 3 tr, ch 5, sc) in next ch-5 sp, (4 dc, 3 tr) in next ch-5 sp.

Motif 3

RND 1: Rep Rnd 1 of Motif 2.

RND 2: Sc in same ch-2 sp, (4 dc, 3 tr) in next ch-5 sp, sl st in adjacent ch-5 sp on Motif 1.

Motif 4

RND 1: Rep Rnd 1 of Motif 2.

RND 2: Sc in same ch-2 sp, (4 dc, 3 tr) in next ch-5 sp, sl st in adjacent ch-4 sp on Motif 1, ch 4, sc in same ch-5 sp on current motif, (4 dc, 3 tr) in next ch-5 sp.

Special Stitch

Picot: Ch 3, sl st in 4th ch from hook.

Motif 5

RND 1: Rep Rnd 1 of Motif 2.

RND 2: Sc in same ch-2 sp, (4 dc, 3 tr) in next ch-5 sp, sl st in adjacent ch-5 sp on Motif 1, ch 4, sc in same ch-5 sp on current motif, (4 dc, 3 tr) in next ch-5 sp, sl st in adjacent ch-5 sp on Motif 2.

Motif 6

RND 1: Rep Rnd 1 of Motif 2.

RND 2: Rep Rnd 2 of Motif 2 except you are joining to adjacent ch-5 sp on Motif 2.

Cont as follows to complete more of Rnd 2 of Motifs 5, 4, and 3: ch 4, sc in ch-5 sp, (4 dc, 3 tr, ch 5, sc) in next ch-5 sp, (4 dc, 3 tr) in next ch-5 sp, sl st in first ch of beg ch, ch 4, sc in next ch-5 sp on Motif 4. (4 dc, 3 tr, ch 5, sc) in next ch-5 sp, (4 dc, 3 tr) in next ch-5 sp, sl st in first ch of beg ch, ch 4, sc in next ch-5 sp on Motif 3. (4 dc, 3 tr, ch 5, sc) in next ch-5 sp. (4 dc, 3 tr) in next ch-5 sp.

Motif 7

RNDS 1–2: Rep Rnds 1–2 of Motif 3.

Motif 8

RND 1: Rep Rnd 1 of Motif 2.

RND 2: Sc in same ch-2 sp, (4 dc, 3 tr) in next ch-5 sp, sl st in adjacent ch-4 sp on Motif 3, ch 4, sc in same ch-5 sp on current motif, (4 dc, 3 tr) in next ch-5 sp.

Motif 9

RND 1: Rep Rnd 1 of Motif 2.

RND 2: Sc in same ch-2 sp, (4 dc, 3 tr) in next ch-5 sp, sl st in adjacent ch-4 sp on Motif 4, ch 4, sc in same ch-5 sp on current motif. (4 dc, 3 tr) in next ch-5 sp.

Motif 10

RND 1: Rep Rnd 1 of Motif 2.

RND 2: Sc in same ch-2 sp, (4 dc, 3 tr) in next ch-5 sp, sl st in adjacent ch-4 sp on Motif 9, ch 4, sc in same ch-5 sp on current motif. (4 dc, 3 tr) in next ch-5 sp, sl st in adjacent ch-5 sp on Motif 5.

Motif 11

RND 1: Rep Rnd 1 of Motif 2.

RND 2: Sc in same ch-2 sp, (4 dc, 3 tr) in next ch-5 sp, sl st in adjacent ch-4 sp on Motif 5, ch 4, sc in same ch-5 sp on current motif. (4 dc, 3 tr) in next ch-5 sp, sl st in adjacent ch-5 sp on Motif 6.

Motif 12

RND 1: Rep Rnd 1 of Motif 2.

RND 2: Rep Rnd 2 of Motif 2 except you are joining to adjacent ch-5 sp on Motif 6,

Cont as follows to complete more of Rnd 2 of Motifs 11, 10, 9, 8, and 7: ch 4, sc in ch-5 sp on

STITCH DIAGRAM B

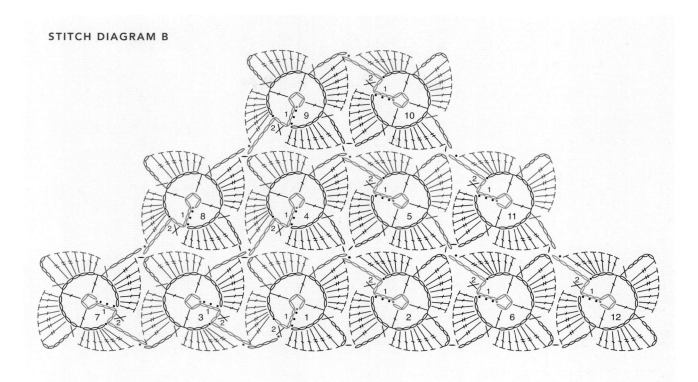

CONSTRUCTION DIAGRAM

						81	82									
					80	64	65	83								
				79	63	49	50	66	84							
			78	62	48	36	37	51	67	85						
		77	61	47	35	25	26	38	52	68	86					
	76	60	46	34	24	16	17	27	39	53	69	87				
75	59	45	33	23	15	9	10	18	28	40	54	70	88			
74	58	44	32	22	14	8	4	5	11	19	29	41	55	71	89	
73	57	43	31	21	13	7	3	1	2	6	12	20	30	42	56	72	90

Motif 11, (4 dc, 3 tr, ch 5, sc) in next ch-5 sp, (4 dc, 3 tr) in next ch-5 sp, sl st in first ch of beg ch on Motif 11, ch 4, sc in ch-5 sp on Motif 10. (4 dc, 3 tr, ch 5, sc) in next ch-5 sp, (4 dc, 3 tr) in next ch-5 sp, sl st in first ch of beg on Motif 10, ch 4, sc in ch-5 sp on Motif 9. (4 dc, 3 tr, ch 5, sc) in next ch-5 sp, (4 dc, 3 tr) in next ch-5 sp, sl st in first ch of beg ch on Motif 9, ch 4, sc in ch-5 sp on Motif 8. (4 dc, 3 tr, ch 5, sc) in next ch-5 sp, (4 dc, 3 tr) in next ch-5 sp, sl st in first ch of beg ch on Motif 8, ch 4, sc in ch-5 sp on Motif 7. (4 dc, 3 tr, ch 5, sc) in next ch-5 sp, (4 dc, 3 tr) in next ch-5 sp.

Motif 13

Rep Rnds 1–2 of Motif 3.

Motifs 14–15

Rep Rnds 1–2 of Motif 8.

Motif 16

Rep Rnds 1–2 of Motif 9.

Motif 17

Rep Rnds 1–2 of Motif 10.

Motifs 18–19

Rep Rnds 1–2 of Motif 11.

Motif 20

Rep Rnds 1–2 of Motif 12.

Completion Row

*Ch 4, sc in ch-5 sp, (4 dc, 3 tr, ch 5, sc) in next ch-5 sp, (4 dc, 3 tr) in next ch-5 sp, sl st in first ch of beg on adjacent motif. Rep from * across to last motif on left side of shawl, omitting last sl st on last motif.

Motifs 21, 31, 43, 57, and 73

Rep Rnds 1–2 of Motif 3.

Motifs 22–24, 32–35, 44–48, 58–63, and 74–80

Rep Rnds 1–2 of Motif 8.

Motifs 25, 36, 49, 64, and 81

Rep Rnds 1–2 of Motif 9.

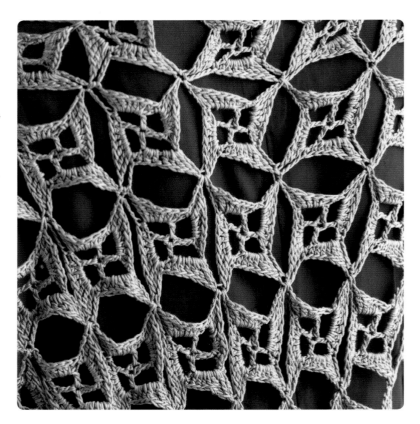

Motif 26, 37, 50, 65, and 82

Rep Rnds 1–2 of Motif 10.

Motifs 27–29, 38–41, 51–55, 66–71, and 83–89

Rep Rnds 1–2 of Motif 11.

Motifs 30, 42, 56, and 72

Rep Rnds 1–2 of Motif 12.

Rep Completion Row after Motifs 30, 42, 56, and 72.

Motif 90

RND 1: Rep Rnd 1 of Motif 2.

RND 2: Sc in same ch-5 sp, (4 dc, 3 tr) in next ch-5 sp, sl st in adjacent ch-5 sp on Motif 72, ch 4, sc in same ch-5 sp on current motif. (4 dc, 3 tr, ch 5, sc) in next ch-5 sp, (4 dc, 3 tr) in next ch-5 sp, ch 14, sl st in 9th ch from hook, (sc, 5 dc, 3 tr, 3 picots, 2 tr, 5 dc, sc) in ch-9 sp, ch 4, sl st in first ch of ch-14, ch 4, sc in same ch-5 sp of current motif, (4 dc, 3 tr) in next ch-5 sp, sl st in first ch of beg ch.

STITCH DIAGRAM C

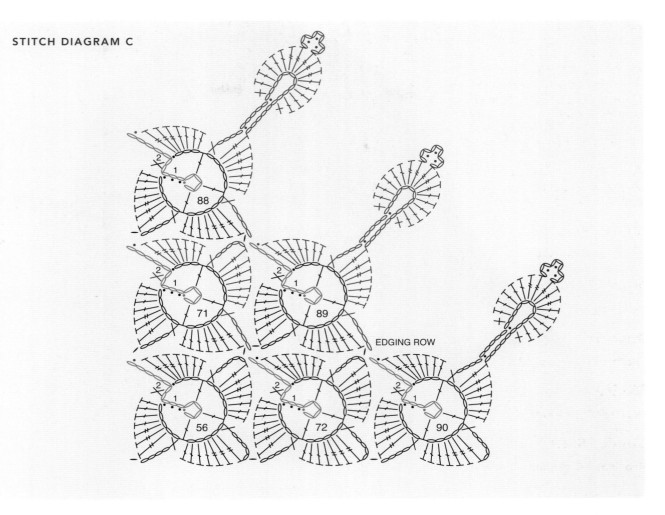

Edging

Refer to Stitch Diagram C above for assistance.

Cont as follows to complete more of Rnd 2 of Motifs 89, 88, 87, 86, 85, 84, 83, 82, 81, 80, 79, 78, 77, 76, 75, 74, and 73: *ch 4, sc in next ch-5 sp on next motif. (4 dc, 3 tr) in next ch-5 sp, ch 14, sl st in 9th ch from hook, (sc, 5 dc, 3 tr, 3 picots, 2 tr, 5 dc, sc) in ch-9 sp, ch 4, sl st in first ch of ch-14, ch 4, sc in same ch-5 sp of current motif, (4 dc, 3 tr) in next ch-5 sp, sl st in first ch of beg ch*. Rep from * to * 7 times (through Motif 82). Ch 14, sl st in 9th ch from hook, (sc, 5 dc, 3 tr, 3 picots, 2 tr, 5 dc, sc) in ch-9 sp, ch 4, sl st in first ch of ch-14, Rep from * to * 9 times, omitting last sl st (through Motif 73). Cont across top edge of shawlette, ch 5, sc in same ch-5 sp, [(4 dc, 3 tr) in next ch-5 sp, sl st in first ch of beg ch, ch 4, sc in next ch-5 sp on next motif] 6 times, (4 dc, 3 tr) in next ch-5 sp,

sl st in first ch of beg ch, ch 4, sl st to first sc on Motif 1. Fasten off. Weave in ends.

Wet block, pin to finished measurements, and let dry.

accessories

The seamless motif accessory collection featured in this chapter runs the gamut from ultra-easy to some more challenging three-dimensional projects. The Radiance Sparkling Skinny Scarf (page 72) is incredibly simple and an extremely quick project that can be whipped up in only a couple of hours. Several hats are also featured, which require a bit more concentration, but will teach you how to join the motif fabric in the round and how to create a three-dimensional project. Each hat features a differently shaped crown and band style. With a little practice, you can create any of these one-skein projects in no time.

snowflake
SCARF

The pretty six-point snowflake motif featured in this elegant scarf is further accentuated with a dainty chain and picot motif that is worked in the large oval space centered between every four motifs. The scarf's length and design make it incredibly versatile: Wear it long to display the pretty stitch work or wrap it loosely around your neck a couple of times for a pretty draped display in front. You can also wear it doubled lengthwise, with the ends threaded through the loop of the opposite end, or as a keyhole scarf by threading one end through a large opening in the lacy stitch work.

YARN

Sportweight (#2 Fine).

shown: The Alpaca Yarn Company, Glimmer (97% baby alpaca/3% polyester; 183 yd [167.3 m]/1.7 oz [50 g]): 3 balls of #1625 icicle.

HOOK

F/5 (3.75mm) or size needed to obtain gauge.

NOTIONS

Tapestry needle for weaving in ends.

GAUGE

1 motif = 5" (12.5 cm) square after blocking.

FINISHED SIZE

10" wide x 85" long (25.5 x 216 cm).

snowflake *motif*

Special Stitches

3 Treble Crochet Cluster (3-tr cl): *Yo twice, insert hook in next st or sp, [yo, pull through 2 loops] twice. Rep from * twice, yo, pull through 4 loops.

4 Treble Crochet Cluster (4-tr cl): *Yo twice, insert hook in next st or sp, [yo, pull through 2 loops] twice. Rep from * 3 times, yo, pull through 5 loops.

Chain-3 Picot (ch-3 picot): Ch 3, sl st in 3rd ch from hook.

Refer to Diagram A above for assistance.

Motif 1A

RND 1: Ch 7 + 4 + 5 + 4 = 20, sl st in 7th ch from hook to form ring. Sl st in ea of next 4 sts (counts as tr), 3-tr cl in ring, [ch 6, 4-tr cl in ring] 5 times, ch 1, sl st in 5th ch of beg ch to join (counts as last ch-6 sp).

RND 2: 7 sc in same ch-6 sp, [ch 9, 7 sc in next ch-6 sp] 5 times, ch 5, sl st in 4th ch of beg ch to join (counts as last ch-9 sp).

RND 3: (Sc, 4 dc, sc) in same ch-9 sp, *sk next sc, sc in ea of next 3 sts, ch-3 picot, sc in ea of next 2 sts, sk next sc, (sc, 4 dc, sc, ch 3, sc, 4 dc, sc) in next ch-9 sp. Rep from * twice. Sk next sc, sc in ea of next 3 sts, ch-3 picot, sc in ea of next 2 sts, sk next sc, (sc, 4 dc, sc), in next ch-9 sp.

Motif 1B

RND 1: Ch 7 + 4 + 5 + 4 + 3 = 23, sl st in 7th ch from hook to form ring. Sl st in ea of next 4 sts (counts as tr), work 3-tr cl in ring, [ch 6, 4-tr cl in ring] 5 times, ch 1, sl st in 5th of beg ch to join (counts as last ch-6 sp).

RND 2: 7 sc in same ch-6 sp, [ch 9, 7 sc in next ch-6 sp] 5 times, ch 5, sl st in 4th ch of beg ch to join (counts as last ch-9 sp).

RND 3: (Sc, 4 dc, sc) in same ch-9 sp, sk next sc, sc in ea of next 3 sts, ch-3 picot, sc in ea of next 2 sts, sk next sc, (sc, 4 dc, sc, ch 1, sl st in ch-3 sp on adjacent motif, ch 1, sc, 4 dc, sc) in next ch-9 sp. *Sk next sc, sc in ea of next 3 sts, ch-3 picot, sc in ea of next 2 sts, sk next sc, (sc, 4 dc, sc, ch 3, sc, 4 dc, sc) in next ch-9 sp. Rep from * once. Sk next sc, sc in ea of next 3 sts, ch-3 picot, sc in ea of next 2 sts, sk next sc, (sc, 4 dc, sc) in next ch-9 sp.

Motif 1C

RNDS 1–2: Rep Rnds 1–2 of Motif 1B.

RND 3: (Sc, 4 dc, sc) in same ch-9 sp, sk next sc, sc in ea of next 3 sts, ch-3 picot, sc in ea of next 2 sts, sk next sc, (sc, 4 dc, sc, ch 1, sl st in ch-3 sp on adjacent motif) in next ch-9 sp, ch 1, sc, 4 dc, sc). *Sk next sc, sc in ea of next 3 sts, ch-3 picot, sc in ea of next 2 sts, sk next sc, (sc, 4 dc, sc, ch 3, sc, 4 dc, sc) in next ch-9 sp. Rep from * 3 times. Sk next sc, sc in ea of next 3 sts, ch-3 picot, sc in ea of next 2 sts, sk next sc, (sc, 4 dc, sc) in next ch-9 sp.

Working across incomplete motifs in row 1, ch 1, sk next ch, sl st in next ch, ch 1, sk next ch, (sc, 4 dc, sc) in next ch-9 sp, skip next sc, sc in each of next 3 sts, ch-3 picot, sc in ea of next 2 sts, (sc, 4 dc, sc, ch 3, sc, 4 dc, sc) in next ch-9 sp, sk next sc, sc in ea of next 3 sts, ch-3 picot, sc in ea of next 2 sts, (sc, 4 dc, sc) in next ch-9 sp, ch 1, sk next ch, sl st in next ch, ch 1, sk next ch, (sc, 4 dc, sc) in next ch-9 sp, sk next sc, sc in ea of next 3 sts, ch-3 picot, sc in ea of next 2 sts, (sc, 4 dc, sc) in next ch-9 sp.

Motif 2A

RNDS 1–2: Rep Rnds 1–2 on Motif 1B.

RND 3: (Sc, 4 dc, sc) in same ch-9 sp, skip next sc, sc in each of next 3 sts, ch-3 picot, sc in ea of next 2 sts, sk next sc, (sc, 4 dc, sc, ch 3, sc, 4 dc, sc) in next ch-9 sp, sk next sc, sc in ea of next 3 sts, ch-3 picot, sc in ea of next 2 sts, sk next st, (sc, 4 dc, sc) in next ch-9 sp.

Motif 2B

RND 1–2: Rep Rnds 1–2 on Motif 1B.

RND 3: (Sc, 4 dc, sc) in same ch-9 sp, *sk next sc, sc in ea of next 3 sts, ch-3 picot, sc in ea of next 2 sts, sk next st, (sc, 4 dc, sc, ch 1, sl st in ch-3 sp on adjacent motif, ch 1, sc, 4 dc, sc) in next ch-9 sp. Rep from * once, sk next sc, sc in ea of next 3 sts, ch-3 picot, sc in ea of next 2 sts, sk next st, (sc, 4 dc, sc, ch 3, sc, 4 dc, sc) in next ch-9 sp, sk next sc, sc in ea of next 3 sts, ch-3 picot, sc in ea of next 2 sts, sk next st, (sc, 4 dc, sc) in next ch-9 sp.

Motif 2C

RNDS 1–2: Rep Rnds 1–2 on Motif 1B.

RND 3: (Sc, 4 dc, sc) in same ch-9 sp, *sk next sc, sc in ea of next 3 sts, ch-3 picot, sc in ea of next 2 sts, sk next st, (sc, 4 dc, sc, ch 1, sl st in ch-3 sp on adjacent motif, ch 1, sc, 4 dc, sc) in next ch-9 sp. Rep from * once, **sk next sc, sc in ea of next 3 sts, ch-3 picot, sc in ea of next 2 sts, sk next st, in next ch-9 sp (sc, 4 dc, sc, ch 3, sc, 4 dc, sc). Rep from ** twice, sk next sc, sc in ea of next 3 sts, ch-3 picot, sc in ea of next 2 sts, sk next st, (sc, 4 dc, sc) in next ch-9 sp.

Working across incomplete motifs in row 2, ch 1, sk next ch, sl st in next ch, ch 1, sk next ch, (sc, 4 dc, sc) in next ch-9 sp, sk next sc, sc in ea of next 3 sts, ch-3 picot, sc in ea of next 2 sts, (sc, 4 dc, sc, ch 3, sc, 4 dc, sc) in next ch-9 sp, sk next sc, sc in ea of next 3 sts, ch-3 picot, sc in ea of next 2 sts, (sc, 4 dc, sc) in next ch-9 sp, ch 1, sk next ch, sl st in next ch, ch 1, sk next ch, (sc, 4 dc, sc) in next ch-9 sp, sk next sc, sc in ea of next 3 sts, ch-3 picot, sc in ea of next 2 sts, (sc, 4 dc, sc) in next ch-9 sp.

Motif 3A

Rep Motif 2A.

Motif 3B

Rep Motif 2B.

Motif 3C

Rep Motif 2C.

Working across incomplete motifs in row 3, *ch 1, sk next ch, sl st in next ch, ch 1, sk next ch, (sc, 4 dc, sc) in next ch-9 sp, sk next sc, sc in ea of next 3 sts, ch-3 picot, sc in ea of next 2 sts, (sc, 4 dc, sc, ch 3, sc, 4 dc, sc) in next ch-9 sp, sk next sc, sc in ea of next 3 sts, ch-3 picot, sc in ea of next 2 sts, (sc, 4 dc, sc) in next ch-9 sp. Rep from * once, ch 3 (sc, 4 dc, sc) in same ch-9 sp, sk next sc, sc in ea of next 3 sts, ch-3 picot, sc in ea of next 2 sts, (sc, 4 dc, sc) in next ch-9 sp.

Working across side edge of incomplete motifs in column A, ch 1, sk next ch, sl st in next ch, ch 1, sk next ch, (sc, 4 dc, sc) in next ch-9 sp, *sk next sc, sc in ea of next 3 sts, ch-3 picot, sc in ea of next 2 sts, sk next st, (sc, 4 dc, sc, ch 3, sc, 4 dc, sc) in next ch-9 sp. Rep from * once, sk next sc, sc in ea of next 3 sts, ch-3 picot, sc in ea of next 2 sts, sk next st, (sc, 4 dc, sc) in next ch-9 sp, ch 1, sk next ch, sl st in next ch, ch 1, sk next ch, (sc, 4 dc, sc) in next ch-9 sp, sk next sc, sc in ea of next 3 sts, ch-3 picot, sc in ea of next 2 sts, sk next st, (sc, 4 dc, sc, ch 3) in next ch-9 sp, sl st in first sc to join. Fasten off.

Snowflake Scarf

Refer to the instructions for the Snowflake Motif on page 44 for motifs referenced in these instructions; refer to Stitch Diagram B at right for assistance.

Motif 1

Work same as Motif 1A.

Motifs 2–16

Work same as Motif 1B.

Motif 17

Work same as Motif 1C.

Working across incomplete motifs in row 1, *ch 1, sk next ch, sl st in next ch, ch 1, sk next ch, (sc, 4 dc, sc) in next ch-9 sp, sk next sc, sc in ea of next 3 sts, ch-3 picot, sc in ea of next 2 sts, (sc, 4 dc, sc, ch 3, sc, 4 dc, sc) in next ch-9 sp, sk next sc, sc in ea of next 3 sts, ch-3 picot, sc in ea of next 2 sts, (sc, 4 dc, sc) in next ch-9 sp. Rep from * 14 times, ch 1, sk next ch, sl st in next ch, ch 1, sk next ch, (sc, 4 dc, sc) in next ch-9 sp, sk next sc, sc in ea of next 3 sts, ch-3 picot, sc in ea of next 2 sts, (sc, 4 dc, sc) in next ch-9 sp.

Motif 18

Work same as Motif 2A.

Motif 19

RNDS 1–2: Rep Rnds 1–2 of Motif 2A.

RND 3: (Sc, 4 dc, sc) in same ch-9 sp, sk next sc, sc in ea of next 3 sts, ch-3 picot, sc in ea of next 2 sts, sk next st, (sc, 4 dc, sc, ch 1, sl st in ch-3 sp on adjacent motif, ch 1, sc, 4 dc, sc) in next ch-9 sp, sk next sc, sc in ea of next 3 sts, ch-3 picot, sc in ea of next 2 sts, sk next st, (sc, 4 dc, sc, ch 1, sl st in adjacent motif) in next ch-9 sp.

Inner motif joining motifs

2, 1, 18, 19 (in that order):

Ch 7, ch-4 picot, ch 4, sl st in junction bet Motifs 2 and 1, ch 4, sl st in 8th ch from hook, ch-4 picot, ch 7, sl st in junction bet Motifs 1 and 18, ch 7, sl st in 14th ch form hook, ch-4 picot, ch 4, sl st in junction bet Motifs 18 and 19, ch 4, sl st in 8th ch from hook, ch-4 picot, sl st in first ch of next ch-7 loop, ch 7, sl st in junction bet Motifs 19 and 2.

Motif 19 *(continued)*

Ch 1, (sc, 4 dc, sc) in same ch-9 sp, sk next sc, sc in ea of next 3 sts, ch-3 picot, sc in ea of next 2 sts, sk next st, (sc, 4 dc, sc, ch 3, sc, 4 dc, sc) in next ch-9 sp, sk next sc, sc in ea of next 3 sts, ch-3 picot, sc in ea of next 2 sts, sk next st, (sc, 4 dc, sc) in next ch-9 sp.

Motifs 20–33

Rep Motif 19, joining inner motif to adjacent motifs.

Motif 34

RNDS 1–2: Rep Rnds 1–2 on Motif 2.

RND 3: (Sc, 4 dc, sc) in same ch-9 sp, sk next sc, sc in ea of next 3 sts, ch-3 picot, sc in ea of next 2 sts, sk next st, (sc, 4 dc, sc, ch 1, sl st in ch-3 sp on adjacent motif, ch 1, sc, 4 dc, sc) in next ch-9 sp, sk next sc, sc in ea of next 3 sts, ch-3 picot, sc in ea of next 2 sts, sk next st, (sc, 4 dc, sc, ch 1, sl st in adjacent motif) in next ch-9 sp.

Inner motif joining motifs

17, 16, 33, 34 (in that order):

Ch 7, ch-4 picot, ch 4, sl st in junction bet Motifs 17 and 16, ch 4, sl st in 8th ch from hook, ch-4 picot, ch 7, sl st in junction bet Motifs 16 and 33, ch 7, sl st in 14th ch from hook, ch-4 picot, ch 4, sl st in junction bet Motifs 33 and 34, ch 4, sl st in 8th ch from hook, ch-4 picot, sl st in first ch of next ch-7 loop, ch 7, sl st in junction bet Motifs 34 and 17.

Motif 33 *(continued)*

Ch 1, (sc, 4 dc, sc) in same ch-9 sp, *sk next sc, sc in ea of next 3 sts, ch-3 picot, sc in ea of next 2 sts, sk next st, (sc, 4 dc, sc, ch 3, sc, 4 dc, sc) in next ch-9 sp, skip next sc. Rep from * twice, sc in ea of next 3 sts, ch-3 picot, sc in ea of next 2 sts, sk next st, (sc, 4 dc, sc) in next ch-9 sp.

Working across incomplete motifs in row 2, *ch 1, sk next ch, sl st in next ch, ch 1, sk next ch, (sc, 4 dc, sc) in next ch-9 sp, sk next sc, sc in ea of next 3 sts, ch-3 picot, sc in ea of next 2 sts, (sc, 4 dc, sc, ch 3, sc, 4 dc, sc) in next ch-9 sp, sk next sc, sc in ea of next 3 sts, ch-3 picot, sc in ea of next 2 sts, (sc, 4 dc, sc) in next ch-9 sp. Rep from * 15 times, ch 3 (sc, 4 dc, sc) in same ch-9 sp, sk next sc, sc in ea of next 3 sts, ch-3 picot, sc in ea of next 2 sts, (sc, 4 dc, sc, ch 3, sc, 4 dc, sc) in next ch-9 sp, sk next sc, sc in ea of next 3 sts, ch-3 picot, sc in ea of next 2 sts, (sc, 4 dc, sc) in next ch-9 sp.

Working across side edge of incomplete motifs in column A, ch 1, sk next ch, sl st in next ch, ch 1, sk next ch, (sc, 4 dc, sc) in next ch-9 sp, sk next sc, sc in ea of next 3 sts, ch-3 picot, sc in ea of next 2 sts, sk next st, (sc, 4 dc, sc, ch 3) in next ch-9 sp, sl st in first sc to join. Fasten off. Weave in ends.

Wet block, pin to finished measurements, and let dry.

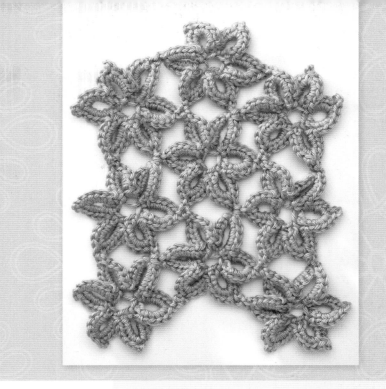

star
MÖBIUS

The star motif featured in this pretty Möbius has an unusual chain center that is easy to crochet and pops open beautifully after blocking. The piece is worked in three colors with contrasting bands at top and bottom, but it would be equally stunning worked in one lush color or in a gradated hue. This Möbius is the perfect accompaniment for many an outfit, worn across the shoulders like a shawlette or around the neck as a scarf/cowl.

YARN

DK weight (#3 Light).

shown: Naturally Caron SPA (75% micro-denier acrylic/25% rayon from bamboo; 251 yd [230 m]/ 3 oz [85 g]): 1 ball ea of #0015 clay pot (A); #0014 rosalinda (B); 0010 stormy blue (C).

HOOK

F/5 (3.75mm) or size needed to obtain gauge.

NOTIONS

Tapestry needle for weaving in ends.

GAUGE

1 motif = 2" (5 cm) wide from side to side; 2½" (6.5 cm) in diameter from point to point.

FINISHED SIZE

20½" wide x 11" long (52 x 28 cm).

star *motif*

STITCH DIAGRAM A

Refer to Stitch Diagram A above for assistance.

Motif 1A

RND 1: Ch 9 + 5 = 14, sl st in 9th ch from hook to form loop, *ch 9, sl st in 9th ch from hook to form loop. Rep from * 3 times. Sl st in sl st at base of first loop, sl st in 5th ch of beg ch to form 6th loop.

RND 2: 5 sc in same ch-9 loop, (5 sc, ch 1, 5 sc) in next loop, 5 sc in next loop.

Motif 1B

RND 1: Rep Rnd 1 of Motif 1A.

RND 2: 5 sc in same ch-9 loop, (5 sc, sl st in ch-1 sp on adjacent motif, 5 sc) in next ch-9 loop. [(5 sc, ch 1, 5 sc) in next loop] twice. 5 sc in next loop.

Motif 1C

RND 1: Rep Rnd 1 of Motif 1A.

RND 2: 5 sc in same ch-9 loop, (5 sc, sl st in ch-1 sp on adjacent motif, 5 sc) in next ch-9 loop. [(5 sc, ch 1, 5 sc) in next loop] 4 times. 5 sc in next loop.

Working across top of incomplete motifs in row 1, *sl st in sp bet this motif and the next motif, 5 sc in next ch-9 loop, (5 sc, ch 1, 5 sc) in next ch-9 sp, 5 sc in next ch-9 loop. Rep from * once.

Motif 2A

RND 1: Rep Rnd 1 of Motif 1A.

RND 2: 5 sc in same ch-9 loop, (5 sc, sl st in ch-1 sp on adjacent motif, 5 sc) in next ch-9 loop, 5 sc in next ch-9 loop.

Motif 2B Rnd 1:

Rep Rnd 1 of Motif 1A.

RND 2: 5 sc in same ch-9 loop. [(5 sc, sl st in next ch-1 sp on adjacent motif, 5 sc) in next ch-9 loop] 3 times, 5 sc in next loop.

Motif 2C

RND 1: Rep Rnd 1 of Motif 1A.

RND 2: 5 sc in same ch-9 loop, [(5 sc, sl st in next ch-1 sp on adjacent motif, 5 sc) in next ch-9 loop] 3 times, [(5 sc, ch 1, 5 sc) in next ch-9 sp] twice, 5 sc in next loop.

Working across top of incomplete motifs in row 2, sl st in sp bet this motif and the next motif, 5 sc in next ch-9 loop. (5 sc, ch 1, 5 sc) in next ch-9 sp, 5 sc in next ch-9 sp. Sl st in sp bet this motif and the next motif, 5 sc in next ch-9 loop, 5 sc in next ch-9 loop.

Motif 3A

RND 1: Rep Rnd 1 of Motif 1A.

RND 2: Work 5 sc in same ch-9 loop, [(5 sc, sl st in next ch-1 sp on adjacent motif, 5 sc) in next ch-9 loop] twice, 5 sc in next ch-9 loop.

Motif 3B

Rep Motif 2B.

Motif 3C

RND 1: Rep Rnd 1 of Motif 1A.

RND 2: 5 sc in same ch-9 loop. [(5 sc, sl st in next ch-1 sp on adjacent motif, 5 sc) in next ch-9 loop] twice [(5 sc, ch 1, 5 sc) in next ch-9 sp] 3 times, 5 sc in next ch-9 loop.

Working across top of incomplete motifs in row 3, sl st in sp bet this motif and the next motif, 5 sc in next ch-9 loop. (5 sc, ch 1, 5 sc) in next ch-9 sp, 5 sc in next ch-9 sp. Sl st in sp bet this motif and the next motif, [(5 sc, ch 1, 5 sc) in next ch-9 sp] twice, 5 sc in next loop.

Working across incomplete motifs in column A, sl st in sp bet this motif and the next motif, 5 sc in next ch-9 loop. [(5 sc, ch 1, 5 sc) in next ch-9 sp] twice, 5 sc in next ch-9 sp. Sl st in sp bet this motif and the next motif, 5 sc in next ch-9 loop, (5 sc, ch 1, 5 sc) in next ch-9 sp, 5 sc in next loop, ch 1, sl st in first sc to join. Fasten off.

Star Motif Möbius

Refer to the instructions for the Star Motif at left for motifs referenced in these instructions; refer to Stitch Diagram B on page 54 for assistance.

Work with yarn color A.

Motif 1

Work same as Motif 1A.

Motifs 2–35

Work same as Motif 1B.

Motif 36

Work same as Motif 1C.

Working across top of incomplete motifs in row 1, *sl st in sp bet this motif and the next, 5 sc in next ch-9 loop, (5 sc, ch 1, 5 sc) in next ch-9 loop, 5 sc in next ch-9 loop. Rep from * 34 times.

Motif 37

Work same as Motif 2A.

Motifs 38–71

Work same as Motif 2B.

Motif 72

Work same as Motif 2C.

Working across top of incomplete motifs in row 2, *sl st in sp bet this motif and the next, 5 sc in next ch-9 loop. (5 sc, ch 1, 5 sc) in next ch-9 loop, 5 sc in next ch-9 loop. Rep from * 33 times. Sl st in sp bet this motif and the next, 5 sc in next motif's ch-9 loop.

Motif 73

Work same as Motif 3A.

Motifs 74–107

Work same as Motif 3B.

Motif 108

Work same as Motif 3C.

Note

The motif should look like a flower with 6 ch-9 petals.

Working across top of incomplete motifs in row 3, *sl st in sp bet this motif and the next motif, 5 sc in next ch-9 loop. (5 sc, ch 1, 5 sc) in next ch-9 loop, 5 sc in next ch-9 loop. Rep from * 33 times. Sl st in sp bet this motif and the next motif, (5 sc, ch 1, 5 sc) in next ch-9 loop.

Note: You will be completing Rnd 2 of the final edge of each row's first motif, while at the same time joining them to the opposite edge of the piece, while twisting the fabric into a möbius strip.

Refer to the Construction Diagram below for assistance.

Fold the fabric in half, folding right-hand side over left-hand side. Take the short edge of top layer and twist it so that row 1 is on top and row 3 is on bottom.

JOINING DIAGRAM

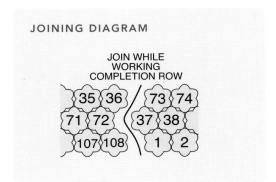

STITCH DIAGRAM B

CONSTRUCTION DIAGRAM
(shows the center color A section; additional rows of motifs are added after joining strip into a möbius)

Complete Rnd 2 of Motifs 73, 37, and 1 and join in a möbius strip as follows: 5 sc in next loop, sl st in ch-1 sp of motif from other end of fabric (Motif 36), 5 sc in same loop on current motif, 5 sc in next loop on current motif, sl st in ch-1 sp on motif from other end of fabric (Motif 36), sl st in first sc of current motif, 5 sc in ea of next 2 loops on Motif 37, sl st in next join on other end of fabric. 5 sc in same loop on Motif 37, 5 sc in next loop, sl st in next join on other end of fabric. 5 sc in same loop, 5 sc in next loop, sl st in ch-1 sp on petal of motif from other end of fabric (Motif 108), sl st in first sc of current motif, 5 sc in same loop, 5 sc in next loop, sl st in ch-1 sp on petal of motif from other end of fabric (Motif 108), 5 sc of same loop, 5 sc in next loop, ch 1, sl st to first sc in Motif 1 to join. Fasten off.

Note: Now that the fabric is twisted into a möbius strip, two rounds of motifs (in colors B and C respectively) will be worked around the edge of the möbius, in one continuous loop that will edge entire perimeter of möbius.

Row 4

Motif 109:

With right side facing, join yarn color B in junction bet any 2 motifs on edge of möbius, work same as Motif 2A.

Motifs 110–215:

Work same as Motif 2B.

Motif 216:

Work same as Motif 2C.

Refer to Joining Diagram on page 54 for assistance.

Completion Rnd:

Working across top of incomplete motifs in row 4, and then joining motifs at beg and end of row together, *sl st in sp bet this motif and the next motif, 5 sc in next ch-9 loop. (5 sc, ch 1, 5 sc) in next ch-9 loop, 5 sc in next ch-9 loop. Rep from * 70 times. Sl st in ch-1 sp on adjacent motif (Motif 180), 5 sc in same ch-9 loop on current motif, (5 sc, sl st in next ch-1 sp on adjacent motif, 5 sc) in next ch-9 loop, 5 sc in next loop, ch 1, sl st in first sc to join. Fasten off B.

Row 5

Motifs 181–252:

With yarn color C, rep Motifs 109–216. Rep Completion Rnd across top of Rnd 5. Fasten off C. Weave in ends.

MODIFICATIONS

This project can easily be modified for a scarf, shawl, or blanket. To preserve a flat fabric, work repeat center motifs in each row for the desired length of fabric, and finish with an end motif.

Based on the yarn, hook, and gauge given on page 51, use these estimates for a scarf, shawl, or blanket as follows:

Scarf: For 80" long x 8" wide (203.5 x 20.5 cm), make 40 motifs per row. Work Row 1 once, rep Rows 2–3 twice, rep Row 2 once.

Shawl: For 72" long x 24" wide (183 x 61 cm), make 36 motifs per row. Work Row 1 once, rep Rows 2–3 five times, rep Row 2 once.

Blanket: For 64" (162.5 cm) square, make 32 motifs per row. Work Row 1 once, rep Rows 2–3 thirty-one times, rep Row 2 once.

lace flower
HAT

The elegant flower motifs used in this lacy hat combine with a pretty scalloped border at the brim to create a stylish accessory. This sample, worked in a silk mohair-blend yarn, is perfect for keeping you toasty warm in cooler weather. Try making one in cotton or linen for a lighter-weight springtime version. The floral openwork stitches up quickly, making this project perfect for a last-minute gift or a swift addition to your wardrobe.

YARN

Dk weight (#3 Light).

shown: S. Charles Collezione, Tivoli (52% silk, 48% kid mohair; 108 yd [100 m/1.75 oz [50 g]) 1 ball #07 amethyst.

HOOK

H/8 (5mm) or size needed to obtain gauge.

NOTIONS

Tapestry needle for weaving in ends.

GAUGE

1 motif = 3" (7.5 cm) after blocking.

FINISHED SIZE

21" (53.5 cm) circumference.

lace flower *motif*

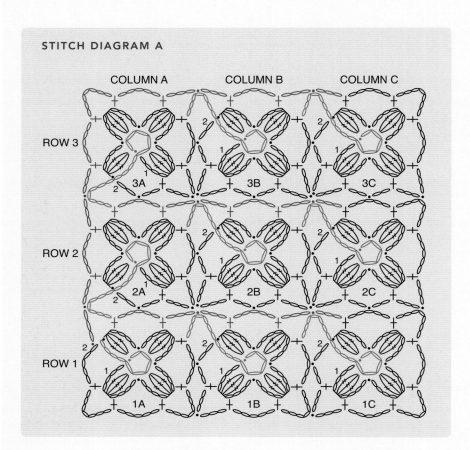

Special Stitch

3 Treble Crochet Cluster

(3-tr cluster): *Yo twice, insert hook in next st or sp, [yo, pull through 2 loops] twice. Rep from * twice (4 loops on hook), yo, pull through all loops.

Refer to Stitch Diagram A above for assistance.

Motif 1A

RND 1: Ch 5 + 4 = 9, sl st in 5th ch from hook to form ring, [ch 4, 3-tr cluster in ring, ch 4, sl st in ring] 3 times, ch 4, 3-tr cluster in ring, sl st to 4th ch of beg ch.

RND 2: Ch 5, sc in next ch-4 sp, ch 7, sc in next ch-4 sp, ch 5, sc in next ch-4 sp.

Motif 1B

RND 1: Ch 5 + 4 + 7 = 16, sl st in 5th ch from hook to form ring, [ch 4, 3-tr cluster in ring, ch 4, sl st in ring] 3 times, ch 4, 3-tr cluster in ring, sl st to 4th ch of beg ch.

RND 2: Ch 2, sl st in ch-5 sp on adjacent motif, ch 2, sc in next ch-4 sp on current motif, ch 3, sl st in 4th ch of ch-7 sp on adjacent motif, ch 3, sc in next ch-4 sp on current motif, ch 5, sc in next ch-4 sp, ch 7, sc in next ch-4 sp, ch 5, sc in next ch-4 sp.

Motif 1C

RND 1: Rep Rnd 1 of Motif 1B.

RND 2: Ch 2, sl st in ch-5 sp on adjacent motif, ch 2, sc in next ch-4 sp on current motif, ch 3, sl st in 4th ch of ch-7 sp on adjacent motif, ch 3, sc in next ch-4 sp on current motif, [ch 5, sc in next ch-4 sp, ch 7, sc in next ch-4 sp] twice, ch 5, sc in next ch-4 sp.

Working across incomplete motifs in row 1, [ch 3, sl st in 4th ch of ch-7, ch 3, sc in next ch-4 sp, ch 5, sc in next ch-4 sp] twice.

Motif 2A

RND 1: Rep Rnd 1 of Motif 1B.

RND 2: Ch 2, sl st in ch-5 sp on adjacent motif, ch 2, sc in next ch-4 sp on current motif, ch 3, sl st in 4th ch of ch-7 sp on adjacent motif, ch 3, sc in next ch-4 sp on current motif, ch 5, sc in next ch-4 sp.

Motif 2B

RND 1: Rep Rnd 1 of Motif 1B.

RND 2: [Ch 2, sl st in ch-5 sp on adjacent motif, ch 2, sc in next ch-4 sp on current motif, ch 3, sl st in 4th ch of ch-7 sp on adjacent motif, ch 3, sc in next ch-4 sp on current motif] twice, ch 5, sc in next ch-4 sp.

Motif 2C

RND 1: Rep Rnd 1 of Motif 1B.

RND 2: [Ch 2, sl st in ch-5 sp on adjacent motif, ch 2, sc in next ch-4 sp on current motif, ch 3, sl st in 4th ch of ch-7 sp on adjacent motif, ch 3, sc in next ch-4 sp on current motif] twice, ch 5, sc in next ch-4 sp, ch 7, sc in next ch-4 sp, ch 5, sc in next ch-4 sp.

Working across incomplete motifs in row 2, [ch 3, sl st in 4th ch of ch-7, ch 3, sc in next ch-4 sp, ch 5, sc in next ch-4 sp] twice.

Motif 3A

Rep Motif 2A.

Motif 3B

Rep Motif 2B.

Motif 3C

Rep Motif 2C.

Working across incomplete motifs in row 3, [ch 3, sl st in 4th ch of ch-7, ch 3, sc in next ch-4 sp, ch 5, sc in next ch-4 sp] twice, ch 7, sc in next ch-4 sp, ch 5, sc in next ch-4 sp.

Working along incomplete motifs in column A, ch 3, sl st in 4th ch of ch-7, ch 3, sc in next ch-4 sp, ch 5, sc in next ch-4 sp, ch 3, sl st in 4th ch of ch-7 sp, ch 3, sl st in first ch of next ch-5 sp. Fasten off.

Lace Flower Hat

Refer to the instructions for the Lace Flower Motif at left for motifs referenced in these instructions; refer to Stitch Diagram B on page 62 for assistance.

Motif 1

Work same as Motif 1A.

Motif 2

Work same as Motif 1B.

Motif 3

Work same as Motif 1C.

Working across incomplete Motifs 3, 2, and 1, [ch 3, sl st in 4th st of ch-7, ch 3, sc in next ch-4 sp, ch 5, sc in next ch-4 sp] twice.

Motif 4

Work same as Motif 2A.

Motif 5

Work same as Motif 2B.

Motif 6

Work same as Motif 2C.

Working across incomplete Motifs 6, 5, and 4, [ch 3, sl st in 4th st of ch-7, ch 3, sc in next ch-4 sp, ch 5, sc in next ch-4 sp] twice.

Motifs 7–20

Rep Motifs 4–6 four times, then rep Motifs 4 and 5 once more.

Notes

This hat is crocheted with a square (4 sided) motif that is converted to a triangle (3 sided) motif for the crown.

The final round is not completed for Motifs 19, 16, 13, 10, 7, 4, and 1 (bottom edge of hat) because the scalloped edge of the exposed flowers makes a pretty and unique brim. If you choose, you can complete the final round of Motifs 19 through 1 and add a different edging for the brim.

STITCH DIAGRAM B

CONTINUE
AT TOP OF
DIAGRAM

Motif 21

Rep Motif 6.

Note: Motifs 22–28 are triangular motifs that will join to Motifs 21–3 (respectively) and to the adjacent triangle motifs (i.e, 22 to 23, 23 to 24, etc.), but the tops will be points. The points will be joined together as a total decrease for the crown. Then, the incomplete sides of Motifs 21, 20, and 19 will be completed as they are simultaneously joined to Motifs 28, 3, 2, and 1 (respectively).

Motif 22

RND 1: Ch 5 + 4 + 7 = 16, sl st in 5th ch from hook to form ring, [ch 4, 3-tr cluster in ring, ch 4, sl st in ring] twice, ch 4, 3-tr cluster in ring, sl st to 4th ch of beg ch.

RND 2: Ch 2, sl st in ch-5 sp on adjacent motif (21), ch 2, sc in next ch-4 sp on current motif, ch 3, sl st in 4th st of ch-7 sp on adjacent motif, ch 3, sc in next ch-4 sp on current motif, ch 5, sc in next ch-4 sp.

Motif 23

RND 1: Rep Rnd 1 of Motif 22.

RND 2: Ch 2, sl st in ch-5 sp on adjacent motif, ch 2, sc in next ch-4 sp on current motif, ch 3, sl st in 4th st of ch-7 sp on adjacent triangle motif, ch 3, sc in next ch-4 sp on current motif, ch 2, sl st in ch-5 sp on adjacent motif, ch 2, sc in next ch-4 sp, ch 3, sl st in 4th st of ch-7 sp on adjacent motif, ch 3, sc in next ch-4 sp, ch 5, sc in next ch-4 sp.

Motifs 24–27

Rep Motif 23 four times.

Motif 28

RND 1: Rep Rnd 1 of Motif 22.

RND 2: Ch 2, sl st in ch-5 sp on adjacent motif, ch 2, sc in next ch-4 sp on current motif, ch 3, sl st in 4th st of ch-7 sp on adjacent motif, ch 3, sc in next ch-4 sp on current motif, ch 2, sl st in ch-5 sp on adjacent motif, ch 2, sc in next ch-4 sp, ch 3, sl st in 4th st of ch-7 sp on adjacent motif, ch 3, sc in next ch-4 sp, ch 5, sc in next ch-4 sp, ch 4, fold hat in half, tr in top of adjacent ch-4 sp at top of motif 22 at opposite end to hat.

Working across Motifs 28, 27, 26, 25, 24, 23, and 22, [insert hook in 4th ch of next ch-7 sp] 6 times, yo, draw yarn through all loops on hook (sl st) to gather all points tog at the top, sl st 3 times across side of last tr made.

Working along side edge of Motifs 22, 21, 20, and 19 while joining them to Motifs 28, 3, 2, and 1 (respectively), sc in top of ch-4 sp on Motif 22, ch 2, sl st in ch-5 sp on Motif 28, ch 2, sc in next ch-4 sp on current motif, ch 3, sl st in 4th st of ch-7 sp and in same position on opposite side of hat bet Motifs 28 and 3, ch 3, sc in next ch-4 sp on Motif 21, ch 2, sl st in ch-5 sp on Motif 3, ch 2, sc in next ch-4 sp on current motif (21), ch 3, sl st in 4th st of ch-7 sp and in same position on adjacent side of hat bet Motifs 3 and 2, ch 3, sc in next ch-4 sp on Motif 20, ch 2, sl st in ch-5 sp on Motif 2, ch 2, sc in next ch-4 sp on current motif (20), ch 3, sl st in 4th st of ch-7 sp and in same position on adjacent side of hat bet Motifs 2 and 1, ch 3, sc in next ch-4 sp on Motif 19, ch 2, sl st in ch-5 sp on Motif 1, ch 2, sl st in next ch-4 sp on current motif (19) ch 7, sl st to top of beg ch-4 on adjacent motif 1. Fasten off. Weave in ends.

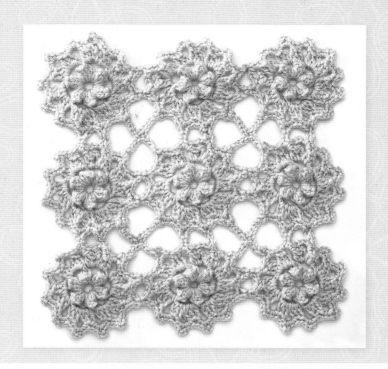

berry blossom
MARKET BAG

I love linen market bags. Linen is so strong, yet it gets softer with every wash. The motif featured in this handy linen bag has popcorn clusters for added texture on the outside of the bag, and there is a secondary small motif worked into the square space centered between every four motifs. It gives the illusion of being worked separately, but is crocheted around the interior edges of the four motifs just as you are joining the fourth motif to the grid. As an added bonus, the gussets and strap are all crocheted right from the motifs. Only the beginning and end yarn tails need be woven into the finished bag.

YARN

Sportweight (#2 Fine).

shown: Louet North America, Euroflax Sport Weight (100% wet-spun linen; 270 yd [247 m]/3.5 oz [100 g]): 2 skeins of #27 crabapple.

HOOK

G/6 (4 mm) or size needed to obtain gauge.

NOTIONS

Tapestry needle for weaving in ends.

GAUGE

1 motif = 5" (12.5 cm) square after blocking.

FINISHED SIZE

The bag is 17" wide x 18" tall (43 x 45.5 cm); total length, including strap, is 36" (91.5 cm).

berry blossom *motif*

STITCH DIAGRAM A

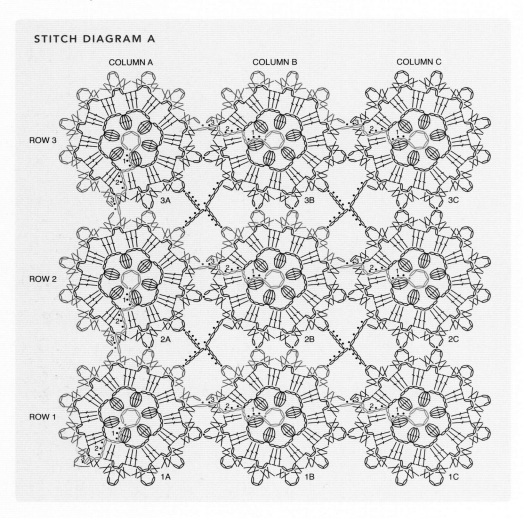

COLUMN A COLUMN B COLUMN C

ROW 3

ROW 2

ROW 1

3A 3B 3C
2A 2B 2C
1A 1B 1C

Special Stitches

Beg Popcorn Stitch (beg popcorn): Sl st in ea of next 3 chs, 4 dc in ring, drop loop from hook, insert hook from front to back in the top of the first dc of group (top of ch-3), pick up dropped loop and pull through.

Popcorn Stitch (popcorn): Work 5 dc in same sp, drop loop from hook, insert hook from front to back in the top of the first dc of group, pick up dropped loop and pull through.

Refer to Stitch Diagram A above for assistance.

Motif 1A

RND 1: Ch 6 + 3 + 3 + 3 + 2 + 1 = 18, sl st to 6th ch from hook to form ring. Beg popcorn in ring, *ch 5, popcorn in ring. Rep from * 4 times, ch 2, sl st to 3rd ch of beg ch (counts as ch-5 sp).

RND 2: Sl st in next 3 chs (counts as dc), 2 dc in next ch-3 sp, *ch 3, (3 dc, ch 3, 3 dc) in next ch-5 sp, rep from * 4 times, 3 dc in next ch-2 sp, ch 1, sl st in 2nd ch from last rnd to join (counts as ch-3 sp).

RND 3: Sl st in next ch, 2 sc in next ch-2 sp, (2 sc, ch 3, 2 sc) in ea of next 4 ch-3 sps, 2 sc in next ch-3 sp.

Motif 1B

RND 1: Ch 6 + 3 + 3 + 3 + 2 + 2 = 19, sl st to 6th ch from hook to form ring. Beg popcorn in ring, *ch 5, popcorn in ring. Rep from * 4 times, ch 2, sl st to 3rd ch of beg ch (counts as ch-5 sp).

RND 2: Rep Rnd 2 of Motif 1A.

RND 3: Sl st in next ch, 2 sc in next ch-2 sp, (2 sc, ch 1, sl st in ch-3 sp of Motif 1A, ch 1, 2 sc) in next ch-3 sp, (2 sc, ch 3, 2 sc) in ea of next 5 ch-3 sps, 2 sc in next ch-3 sp.

Motif 1C

RND 1: Rep Rnd 1 of Motif 1B.

RND 2: Rep Rnd 2 of Motif 1A.

RND 3: Sl st in next ch, 2 sc in next ch-2 sp, (2 sc, ch 1, sl st in ch-3 sp of Motif 1B, ch 1, 2 sc) in next ch-3 sp, (2 sc, ch 3, 2 sc) in ea of next 10 ch-3 sps, 2 sc in next ch-3 sp, ch 1, sk next ch, sl st in next ch.

Working across incomplete motifs in row 1, ch 1, 2 sc in next ch-3 sp, (2 sc, ch 3, 2 sc) in ea of next 4 ch-3 sps, 2 sc in next ch-3 sp, ch 1, sk next ch, sl st in next ch, ch 1, 2 sc in next ch-3 sp, (2 sc, ch 3, 2 sc) in ea of next 2 ch-3 sps, 2 sc in next ch-3 sp.

Motif 2A

RND 1: Rep Rnd 1 of Motif 1B.

RND 2: Rep Rnd 2 of Motif 1A.

RND 3: Sl st in next ch, 2 sc in next ch-2 sp, (2 sc, ch 1, sl st in ch-3 sp of Motif 1A, ch 1, 2 sc) in next ch-3 sp, (2 sc, ch 3, 2 sc) in ea of next 2 ch-3 sps, 2 sc in next ch-3 sp.

Motif 2B

RND 1: Rep Rnd 1 of Motif 1B.

RND 2: Rep Rnd 2 of Motif 1A.

RND 3: Sl st in next ch, 2 sc in same ch-3 sp, (2 sc, ch 1, sl st in Motif 2A ch-3 sp, ch 1, 2 sc) in next ch-3 sp, 2 sc in next ch-3 sp, ch 2.

Inner motif joining motifs

1B, 1A, 2A, 2B (in that order):

Ch 8, sl st in ch-3 sp on Motif 1B, turn, sl st in ea of next 4 chs, ch 4, sl st in ch-3 sp on Motif 1A, sl st in ea of next 4 chs, ch 4, sl st in ch-3 sp on Motif 2A, sl st in ea of next 8 chs, ch 1, 2 sc in same ch-3 sp on Motif 2B.

RND 3 (CONT): *(2 sc, ch 1, sl st in ch-3 sp on adjacent Motif 1B, ch 1, 2 sc) in next ch-3 sp. Rep from * once, (2 sc, ch 3, 2 sc) in ea of next 2 ch-3 sps, 2 sc in next ch-3 sp.

Motif 2C

RND 1: Rep Rnd 1 of Motif 1B.

RND 2: Rep Rnd 2 of Motif 1A.

RND 3: Sl st in next ch, 2 sc in same ch-3 sp, (2 sc, ch 1, sl st in Motif 2A ch-3 sp, ch 1, 2 sc) in next ch-3 sp, 2 sc in next ch-3 sp, ch 2.

Inner motif joining motifs

1C, 1B, 2B, 2C (in that order):

Ch 8, sl st in ch-3 sp on Motif 1C, turn, sl st in ea of next 4 chs, ch 4, sl st in ch-3 sp on Motif 1B, sl st in ea of next 4 chs, ch 4, sl st in ch-3 sp on Motif 2B, sl st in ea of next 8 chs, ch 1, 2 sc in same ch-3 sp on Motif 2C.

RND 3 (CONTINUED): *(2 sc, ch 1, sl st in ch-3 sp on adjacent Motif 1C, ch 1, 2 sc) in next ch-3 sp. Rep from * once, (2 sc, ch 3, 2 sc) in ea of next 7 ch-3 sps, 2 sc in next ch-3 sp, ch 1, sk next ch, sl st in next ch.

Working across incomplete motifs in row 2, ch 1, 2 sc in next ch-3 sp, (2 sc, ch 3, 2 sc) in ea of next 4 ch-3 sps, 2 sc in next ch-3 sp, ch 1, sk next ch, sl st in next ch, ch 1, 2 sc in next ch-3 sp, (2 sc, ch 3, 2 sc) in ea of next 2 ch-3 sps, 2 sc in next ch-3 sp.

Motif 3A

Rep Motif 2A.

Motif 3B

Rep Motif 2B.

Motif 3C

Rep Motif 2C.

Working across incomplete motifs in Row 3, ch 1, 2 sc in next ch-3 sp, (2 sc, ch 3, 2 sc) in ea of next 4 ch-3 sps, 2 sc in next ch-3 sp, ch 1, sk next ch, sl st in next ch, ch 1, 2 sc in next ch-3 sp, (2 sc, ch 3, 2 sc) in ea of next 7 ch-3 sps, 2 sc in next ch-3 sp, ch 1, sk next ch, sl st in next ch.

Working down side edge of incomplete motifs in column A, ch 1, 2 sc in next ch-3 sp, (2 sc, ch 3, 2 sc) in ea of next 4 ch-3 sps, 2 sc in next ch-3 sp, ch 1, sk 1 ch, sl st in next ch, ch 1, 2 sc in next ch-3 sp, (2 sc, ch 3, 2 sc) in ea of next 3 ch-3 sps, 2 sc in last ch-3 sp, ch 1, hdc in first sc on Motif 1A. Fasten off.

Berry Blossom Market Bag

Refer to the instructions for the Berry Blossom Motif on page 66 for motifs referenced in these instructions; refer to Stitch Diagram B at right for assistance.

Motif 1

Work same as Motif 1A.

Motifs 2–7

Work same as Motif 1B.

Motif 8

Work same as Motif 1C.

Working across incomplete motifs in first row of motifs, *ch 1, 2 sc in next ch-3 sp, (2 sc, ch 3, 2 sc) in ea of next 4 ch-3 sps, 2 sc in next ch-3 sp, ch 1, sk next ch, sl st in next ch. Rep from * 5 times, ch 1, 2 sc in next ch-3 sp, (2 sc, ch 3, 2 sc) in ea of next 2 ch-3 sps, 2 sc in next ch-3 sp.

Motif 9

Work same as Motif 2A.

Motifs 10–15

Work same as Motif 2B.

Motif 16

Work same as Motif 2C.

Working across incomplete motifs in 2nd row of motifs, *ch 1, 2 sc in next ch-3 sp, (2 sc, ch 3, 2 sc) in ea of next 4 ch-3 sps, 2 sc in next ch-3 sp, ch 1, sk next ch, sl st in next ch. Rep from * 5 times, ch 1, 2 sc in next ch-3 sp, (2 sc, ch 3, 2 sc) in ea of next 2 ch-3 sps, 2 sc in next ch-3 sp.

Motifs 17–24

Rep Motifs 9–16.

Working across incomplete motifs in 3rd row of motifs, *ch 1, 2 sc in next ch-3 sp, (2 sc, ch 3, 2 sc) in ea of next 4 ch-3 sps, 2 sc in next ch-3 sp, ch 1, sk next ch, sl st in next ch, ch 1, rep from * 5 times, ch 1, 2 sc in next ch-3 sp, (2 sc, ch 3, 2 sc) in ea of next 7 ch-3 sps, 2 sc in next ch-3 sp, ch 1, sk next ch, sl st in next ch.

Note

Winding linen yarn a couple of times before crocheting will soften it up considerably.

Special Stitches

Refer to Special Stitches on page 66 for instructions on other special stitches used in this pattern.

Dtr10tog: [Yo 3 times, insert hook in next st or sp, yo, draw through st, (yo, draw yarn through 2 loops) 3 times] 10 times, yo, draw yarn through 11 loops on hook to complete dtr10tog.

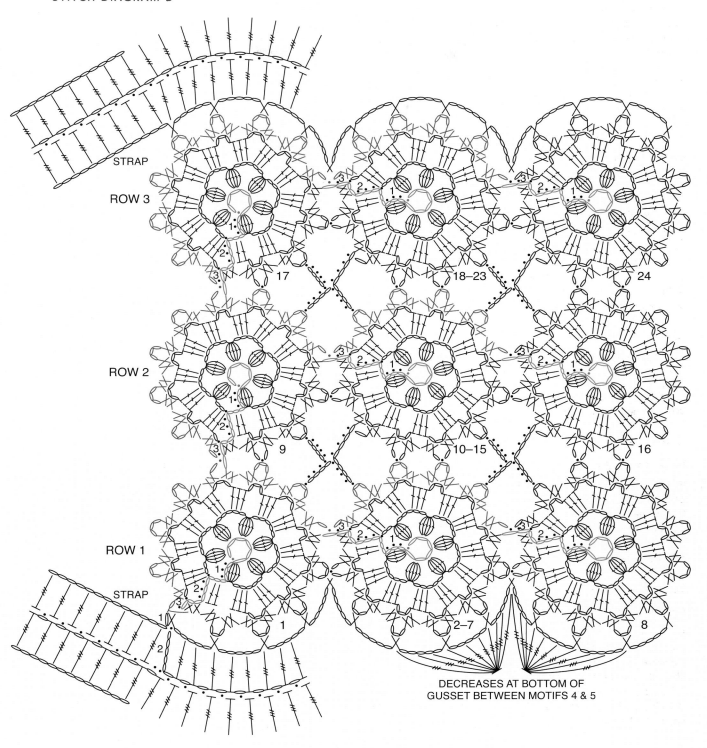

ROW 3

ROW 2

ROW 1

STRAP

STRAP

17

18–23

24

9

10–15

16

1

2–7

8

DECREASES AT BOTTOM OF
GUSSET BETWEEN MOTIFS 4 & 5

Working down side edge of incomplete motifs in column A, *ch 1, 2 sc in next ch-3 sp, (2 sc, ch 3, 2 sc) in ea of next 4 ch-3 sps, 2 sc in next ch-3 sp, ch 1, sk 1 ch, sl st in next ch, ch 1, 2 sc in next ch-3 sp, (2 sc, ch 3, 2 sc) in ea of next 3 ch-3 sps, 2 sc in last ch-3 sp, ch 1, hdc in first sc on Motif 1. Do not fasten off.

Side Gusset and Strap

Note: The strap and both side gussets are worked in one piece, while joining the motif fabric simultaneously.

RND 1: Ch 1, sc in same ch-3 sp on corner of Motif 1, **[ch 5, sc in next ch-3 sp] 3 times, *ch 5, sc in junction bet motifs, [ch 5, sc in next ch-3 sp] 4 times, rep from * 5 times, ch 5, sc in junction bet motifs, [ch 5, sc in next ch-3 sp] 4 times, ch 72**, sk rem 3 ch-3 sps at end of Motif 8, 4 ch-3 sps at end of Motif 16 and next 3 ch-3 sps at end of Motif 24, sc in next corner ch-3 on Motif 24. Rep from ** to ** once, sl st in top of sc at beg of rnd—two 72-ch lengths; 76 ch-5 sps.

RND 2: Ch 6 (counts as dtr, ch 1), ***[(dtr, ch 1, dtr, ch 1) in next ch-5 sp, dtr in next sc, ch 1] 15 times, [dtr, ch 1] twice in next ch-5 sp, work dtr10tog over next 3 ch-5 sps as follows: *[next leg in next sc, 2 legs in next ch-5 sp] 3 times, next leg in next sc, complete dtr10tog*. Starting in same sc as last leg, rep from * to * once, fold bag in half and join front to back while working remainder of gusset, **[sl st in corresponding ch-1 sp on opposite side of gusset, dtr in next ch-5 sp] twice, sl st in corresponding ch-1 sp on opposite side of gusset, dtr in next sc, rep from ** 15 times ***. Working across long ch, sk next ch, [dtr in next ch, ch 1, sk next ch] 36 times, dtr in next sc on Motif 24, ch 1, rep from *** to *** once, working across long ch, sk next ch, [dtr in next ch, sl st in corresponding ch-1 sp on opposite side of strap, sk next ch] 36 times, join with sl st in 5th ch of beg ch-6.

Fasten off. Weave in loose ends.

Wet block to finished measurements and let dry.

Note: Due to the nature of the linen fiber, the bag will get softer with each wash while maintaining its strength and durability.

radiance
SPARKLY SKINNY SCARF

This super-simple flower motif really opens up beautifully when blocked. It would make a great belt/sash, purse handle, headband, bracelet, or scarf—depending on the yarn, gauge, and length you choose. For the sample shown here, I used a sparkly beaded yarn and crocheted a long piece to create a skinny scarf. The scarf is delicate and sophisticated, with a jewelry-like appeal. Pair it with a pretty evening ensemble or use it to enhance a plain top for work. Wear it long or wind it loosely around your neck to create a multistrand "necklace."

YARN

Laceweight (#0 Lace).

shown: Tilli Tomas, Symphony Lace with Beads and Glitter (63% kid mohair, 10% silk, 18% nylon, 9% wool; 345 yd [315 m]/ 3.5 oz [100 g]): 1 skein of coral sap (deep pink).

HOOK

G/6 (4 mm) or size needed to obtain gauge.

NOTIONS

Tapestry needle for weaving in ends.

GAUGE

1 motif = 2" (5 cm) diameter after blocking.

FINISHED SIZE

2" wide x 80" long (5 x 203.5 cm).

radiance *motif*

STITCH DIAGRAM A

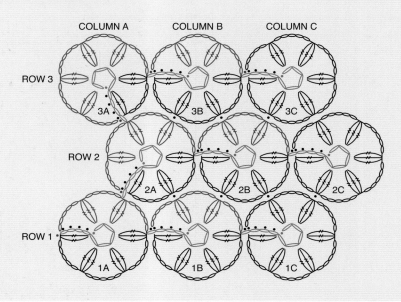

STITCH DIAGRAM A

COLUMN A   COLUMN B   COLUMN C

ROW 3   3A   3B   3C

ROW 2   2A   2B   2C

ROW 1   1A   1B   1C

Special Stitches

2 Treble Crochet Cl (2-tr cl): *Yo twice, insert hook in next st or sp, [yo, pull through 2 loops] twice. Rep from * once (3 loops on hook), yo, pull through all loops.

3 Treble Crochet Cl (3-tr cl): *Yo twice, insert hook in next st or sp, [yo, pull through 2 loops] twice. Rep from * twice (4 loops on hook), yo, pull through all loops.

Refer to Stitch Diagram A above for assistance.

Motif 1A

RND 1: Ch 5 + 4 = 9, sl st in 5th ch from hook to form ring, sl st in ea of next 4 chs (counts as tr), 2-tr cl in ring, *ch 5, 3-tr cl in ring. Rep from * twice.

Motif 1B

Rep Motif 1A.

Motif 1C

RND 1: Ch 5 + 4 = 9, sl st in 5th ch from hook to form ring, sl st in ea of next 4 chs (counts as tr), 2-tr cl in ring, *ch 5, 3-tr cl in ring. Rep from * 4 times, ch 5, sl st in sp before next motif.

Working across incomplete motifs in Row 1, [ch 5, 3-tr cl in ring on Motif 1B] twice, ch 5, sl st in sp before next motif, ch 5, 3-tr cl in ring on Motif 1A.

Motif 2A

RND 1: Ch 5 + 4 = 9, sl st in 5th ch from hook to form ring, sl st in ea of next 4 chs (counts as tr), work 2-tr cl in ring, *ch 5, 3-tr cl in ring*, sl st in corresponding cl on adjacent motif. Rep from * to * once.

Motif 2B

RND 1: Ch 5 + 4 = 9, sl st in 5th ch from hook to form ring, sl st in ea of next 4 chs (counts as tr), 2-tr cl in ring, *ch 5, 3-tr cl in ring**, sl st in corresponding cl on Motif 1B*. Rep from * to * once. Rep from * to ** once.

Motif 2C

RND 1: Ch 5 + 4 = 9, sl st in 5th ch from hook to form ring, sl st in ea of next 4 chs (counts as tr), 2-tr cl in ring, *ch 65, 3-tr cl in ring*, sl st in corresponding cl on adjacent motif. Rep from * to * once, 4 times, ch 5, sl st in sp before next motif.

Working across incomplete motifs in Row 2, [ch 5, 3-tr cl in ring on Motif 2B] twice, ch 5, sl st in sp before next motif, [ch 5, 3-tr cl in ring on Motif 2A] twice.

Motif 3A

RND 1: Ch 5 + 4 = 9, sl st in 5th ch from hook to form ring, sl st in ea of next 4 chs (counts as tr), 2-tr cl in ring, ch 5, 3-tr cl in ring.

Motif 3B

RND 1: Ch 5 + 4 = 9, sl st in 5th ch from hook to form ring, sl st in ea of next 4 chs (counts as tr), 2-tr cl in ring, *ch 5, 3tr-cl in ring**, sl st in corresponding cl on adjacent motif*. Rep from * to * once. Rep from * to ** once.

Motif 3C

RND 1: Ch 5 + 4 = 9, sl st in 5th ch from hook to form ring, sl st in ea of next 4 chs (counts as tr), 2-tr cl in ring, *ch 5, 3tr-cl in ring**, sl st in corresponding cl on adjacent motif*. Rep from * to * once. Rep from * to ** 3 times, ch 5, sl st in sp before next motif.

Working across incomplete motifs in Row 3, [ch 5, 3-tr cl in ring on Motif 3B] twice, ch 5, sl st in sp before next motif, [ch 5, 3-tr cl in ring on Motif 3A] 4 times, ch 5.

Working along side edge of incomplete motifs in column A, sl st in sp before next motif, ch 5, 3-tr cl in ring on Motif 2A, ch 5, sl st in sp before next motif, ch 5, 3-tr cl in ring on Motif 1A, ch 5, sl st to top of ch-4 at beg of rnd to join. Fasten off.

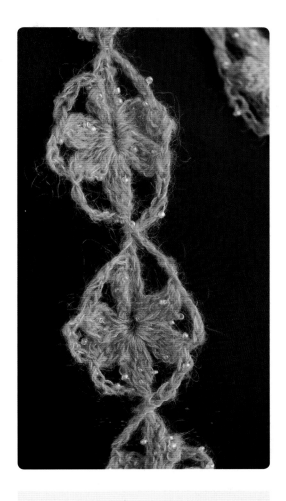

Note

This pattern is very versatile. Try making a sash by using a sturdier yarn and tight gauge. For a bracelet, use a stretchy yarn and create a tube or crochet flat and secure with jewelry findings.

Refer to Special Stitches on page 74 for special stitches used in this pattern.

Radiance Sparkling Skinny Scarf

Refer to Stitch Diagram B at right for assistance. Radiance Motif instructions begin on page 74.

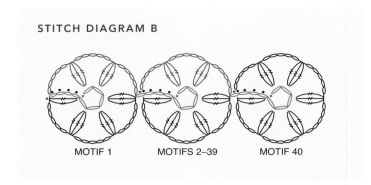

STITCH DIAGRAM B

MOTIF 1   MOTIFS 2–39   MOTIF 40

Motif 1

RND 1: Ch 5 + 4 = 9, sl st in 5th ch from hook to form ring, sl st in each of next 4 chs (counts as tr), 2-tr cl in ring, *ch 5, 3-tr cl in ring. Rep from * twice.

Motifs 2–39

Rep Motif 1.

Motif 40

RND 1: Ch 5 + 4 = 9, sl st in 5th ch from hook to form ring, sl st in each of next 4 chs (counts as tr), 2-tr cl in ring, *ch 5, 3-tr cl in ring. Rep from * 4 times, ch 5, sl st in sp before next motif.

Working across incomplete motifs in row 1, *[ch 5, 3-tr cl in ring on next motif] twice, ch 5, sl st in sp before next motif. Rep from * to complete each motif across to Motif 1, ch 5, 3-tr cl in ring on Motif 1, ch 5, sl st in top of ch-4 at beg of rnd to join. Fasten off. Weave in ends.

Steam block, pin to finished measurements to open up the flower motifs, and let dry.

Note: Due to the delicate nature of the beads and mohair, steam blocking is best for this project.

blue skies
CHUNKY COWL

Named after the beautiful Willie Nelson song, this soft, chunky cowl is the perfect accessory for a blustering, snowy day. The cowl is warm and cozy and will add a pop of color and a graphic appeal to your favorite sweater or jacket. The one-round disc motifs are ultra simple and the bulky yarn and large hook make this a really quick project. As a one-size-fits-most project, this would be a great gift or a fabulous donation to charity.

YARN

Bulky weight (#6 Super Bulky).

shown: Lion Brand, Hometown USA (100% acrylic; 81 yd [74 m]/5 oz [142 g]): 2 balls of #107 charlotte blue.

HOOK

10 mm or size needed to obtain gauge.

NOTIONS

Tapestry needle for weaving in ends.

GAUGE

1 motif = 2½" (6.5 cm) in diameter.

FINISHED SIZE

13½" wide x 12½" tall (34.5 x 31.5 cm).

blue skies *motif*

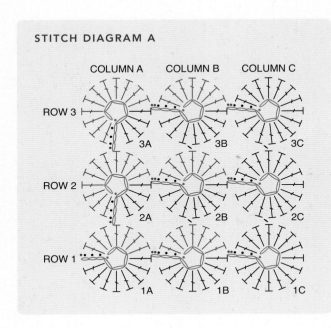

STITCH DIAGRAM A

Refer to Stitch Diagram A above for assistance.

Motif 1A

RND 1: Ch 5 + 3 = 8, sl st in 5th ch from hook to form ring, sl st in ea of next 3 chs (counts as dc), 8 dc in ring.

Motif 1B

Rep Rnd 1 of Motif 1A.

Motif 1C

RND 1: Ch 5 + 3 = 8, sl st in 5th ch from hook to form ring, sl st in each of next 3 chs (counts as dc), 15 dc in ring.

Working across incomplete motifs of row 1, sl st in sp before next motif, 7 dc in next ring, sl st in sp before next motif, work 4 dc in next ring.

Motif 2A

RND 1: Ch 5 + 3 = 8, sl st in 5th ch from hook to form ring, sl st in ea of next 3 chs (counts as dc), 4 dc in ring.

Motif 2B

RND 1: Ch 5 + 3 = 8, sl st in 5th ch from hook to form ring, sl st in ea of next 3 chs (counts as dc), 3 dc in ring, sl st to top of motif in row below, 5 dc in ring.

Motif 2C

RND 1: Ch 5 + 3 = 8, sl st in 5th ch from hook to form ring, sl st in ea of next 3 chs (counts as dc), 3 dc in ring, sl st to top of motif in row below, 12 dc in ring.

Working across incomplete motifs of row 2, sl st in top of ch-3 at beg of rnd, sl st in sp before next motif, 7 dc in next ring, sl st in sp before next motif, 4 dc in next ring.

Motif 3A

Rep Motif 2A.

Motif 3B

Rep Motif 2B.

Motif 3C

Rep Motif 2C.

Working across incomplete motifs of row 3, sl st in top of ch-3 at beg of rnd, sl st in sp before next motif, 7 dc in next ring, sl st in sp before next motif, work 11 dc in next ring.

Working across side edge of motifs in column A, sl st in top of ch-3 at beg of rnd, sl st in sp before next motif, 7 dc in next ring, sl st in top of ch-3 at beg of rnd, sl st in sp before next motif, 3 dc in next ring, sl st to top of ch-3 at beg of round to join. Fasten off.

Note

For a slightly different look, work the fabric flat (not joined in a tube) and find a large interesting button for a closure. Wrap around your neck and secure with the button just offset from the center front.

Blue Skies Cowl

Refer to the instructions for the Blue Skies Motif at left for motifs referenced in these instructions; refer to Stitch Diagram B on page 82 for assistance.

Motif 1

Work same as Motif 1A.

Motifs 2–10

Work same as Motif 1B.

Motif 11

Work same as Motif 1C.

Working across incomplete Motifs 10–1, *sl st in top of ch-3 at beg of rnd, sl st in sp before next motif, 7 dc in next ring. Rep from * 8 times, sl st in sp before Motif 1, 4 dc in next ring.

Motif 12

Work same as Motif 2A.

Motifs 13–21

Work same as Motif 2B.

Motif 22

Work same as Motif 2C.

Completion Row

Working across incomplete Motifs 21–12, sl st in top of ch-3 at beg of rnd, sl st in sp before next motif, work 8 more dc in next ring. Rep from * 8 times, sl st in sp before next motif, 4 dc in next ring.

Motifs 23–44

Rep Motifs 12–22 and Completion Row (twice).

Motifs 45–55

Rep Motifs 12–22.

Completion Row

Working across incomplete Motifs 54–45, sl st in top of ch-3 at beg of rnd, sl st in sp before next motif, work 7 dc in next ring. Rep from * 9 times.

Working across incomplete Motifs 45, 34, 23, 12 and 1, while at the same time, joining them to Motifs 55, 44, 33, 22, 11 to form a tube (cowl), sl st in side of Motif 55, work 4 more dc in Motif 45, sl st in top of ch-3 at beg of rnd, sl st in sp before next motif, work 3 dc in next ring, sl st to side of Motif 44, work 4 dc in ring, sl st in top of ch-3 at beg of rnd, sl st in sp before next motif, work 3 dc in next ring, sl st in side of Motif 33, work 4 dc in ring, sl st in sp before Motif 12, work 3 dc in next ring, sl st to side of Motif 22, work 4 dc in ring, sl st in top of ch-3 at beg of rnd, sl st in sp before Motif 1, work 3 dc in next ring, sl st to side of Motif 11, sl st to top of ch-3 at beg of Motif 1. Fasten off. Weave in ends.

STITCH DIAGRAM B

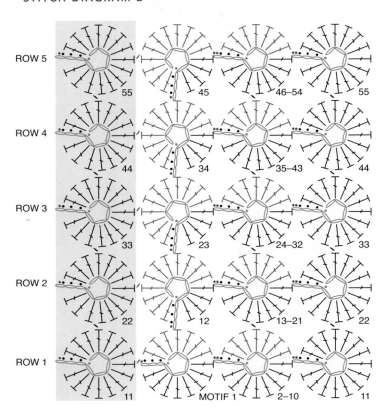

jamie
HAT

This hat uses a simple square shape to create a streamlined design that will be a welcome gift for the special man in your life. In this hat, a traditional square motif is used, which is converted to a hexagon to shape the top of the hat (or crown). To make this hat work for a woman, simply choose a pretty feminine yarn color; it will change the look of the hat dramatically without changing the motif or construction!

YARN

Worsted weight (#4 Medium).

shown: Stitch Nation by Debbie Stoller (division of Red Heart), Bamboo Ewe (55% viscose from bamboo/45% wool; 177 yd [162 m]/ 3.5 oz [100 g]): 1 ball of #5410 mercury.

HOOK

F/5 (3.75mm) or size needed to obtain gauge.

NOTIONS

Tapestry needle for weaving in ends.

GAUGE

1 motif = 3¼" (8.5 cm) square.

FINISHED SIZE

19½" (49.5 cm) in circumference unstretched.

jamie *motif*

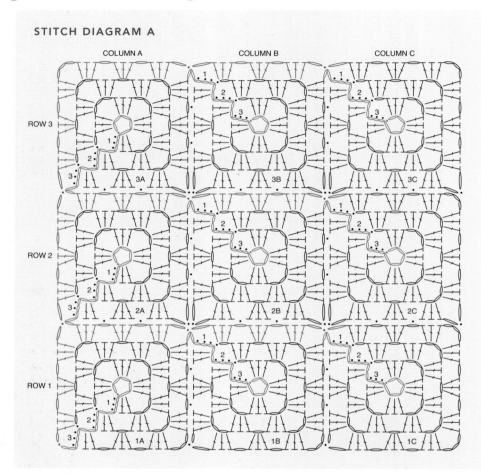

STITCH DIAGRAM A

COLUMN A   COLUMN B   COLUMN C

ROW 3

ROW 2

ROW 1

3A   3B   3C

2A   2B   2C

1A   1B   1C

Motif 1A

Refer to Stitch Diagram A above for assistance.

RND 1: Ch 5 + 3 + 2 + 3 + 2 + 3 + 2 = 20, sl st in 5th ch from hook to form ring, sl st in ea of next 3 chs (counts as dc), 2 dc in same ring, [ch 3, 3 dc] 3 times in same ring, ch 1, sl st to 2nd ch of beg ch (counts as ch-3).

RND 2: Sl st in ea of next 3 chs (counts as dc), 2 dc in same ch-3 sp, [ch 1, (3 dc, ch 3, 3 dc) in next ch-3 sp] 3 times, ch 1, 3 dc in next ch-3 sp, ch 1, sl st to 2nd ch of beg ch (counts as ch-3).

RND 3: Sl st in ea of next 3 chs (counts as dc), 2 dc in same ch-3 sp, ch 1, 3 dc in next ch-1 sp, ch 1, (3 dc, ch 3, 3 dc) in next ch-3 sp, ch 1, 3 dc in next ch-1 sp, ch 1, 3 dc in next ch-3 sp.

Motif 1B

RNDS 1–2: Rep Rnds 1–2 of Motif 1A.

RND 3: Sl st in ea of next 3 chs (counts as dc), 2 dc in same ch-3 sp, sl st in ch-1 sp on adjacent motif, 3 dc in next ch-1 sp, sl st in next ch-1 sp on adjacent motif, (3 dc, ch 1, sl st in ch-3 sp on adjacent motif, ch 1, 3 dc) in next ch-3 sp, ch 1, 3 dc in next ch-1 sp, ch 1, (3 dc, ch 3, 3 dc) in next ch-3 sp, ch 1, 3 dc in next ch-1 sp, ch 1, 3 dc in next ch-3 sp.

Motif 1C

RNDS 1–2: Rep Rnds 1–2 of Motif 1A.

RND 3: Sl st in ea of next 3 chs (counts as dc), 2 dc in same ch-3 sp, sl st in ch-1 sp on adjacent motif, 3 dc in next ch-1 sp, sl st in next ch-1 sp on adjacent motif, (3 dc, ch 1, sl st in ch-3 sp on adjacent motif, ch 1, 3 dc) in next ch-3 sp, [ch 1, 3 dc in next ch-1 sp, ch 1, (3 dc, ch 3, 3 dc) in next ch-3 sp] twice, ch 1, 3 dc in next ch-1 sp, ch 1, 3 dc in next ch-3 sp.

Working across incomplete motifs in row 1, [ch 1, sl st in 2nd ch of ch-2 sp, ch 1, 3 dc in next ch-3 sp on next motif, ch 1, 3 dc in next ch-1 sp, ch 1, 3 dc in next ch-3 sp] twice.

Motif 2A

RNDS 1–2: Rep Rnds 1–2 of Motif 1A.

RND 3: Sl st in ea of next 3 chs (counts as dc), 2 dc in same ch-3 sp, sl st in ch-1 sp on adjacent motif, 3 dc in next ch-1 sp, sl st in next ch-1 sp on adjacent motif, (3 dc, ch 1, sl st in ch-3 sp on adjacent motif, ch 1, 3 dc) in next ch-3 sp, ch 1, 3 dc in next ch-1 sp, ch 1, 3 dc in next ch-3 sp.

Motif 2B

RNDS 1–2: Rep Rnds 1–2 of Motif 1A.

RND 3: Sl st in ea of next 3 chs (counts as dc), 2 dc in same ch-3 sp, [sl st in ch-1 sp on adjacent motif, 3 dc in next ch-1 sp, sl st in next ch-1 sp on adjacent motif, (3 dc, ch 1, sl st in ch-3 sp on adjacent motif, ch 1, 3 dc) in next ch-3 sp] twice, ch 1, 3 dc in next ch-1 sp, ch 1, 3 dc in next ch-3 sp.

Motif 2C

RNDS 1–2: Rep Rnds 1–2 of Motif 1A.

RND 3: Sl st in ea of next 3 chs (counts as dc), 2 dc in same ch-3 sp, [sl st in ch-1 sp on adjacent motif, 3 dc in next ch-1 sp, sl st in next ch-1 sp on adjacent motif, (3 dc, ch 1, sl st in ch-3 sp on adjacent motif, ch 1, 3 dc) in next ch-3 sp] twice, ch 1, 3 dc in next ch-1 sp, ch 1, (3 dc, ch 3, 3 dc) in next ch-3 sp, ch 1, 3 dc in next ch-1 sp, ch 1, 3 dc in next ch-3 sp.

Working across incomplete motifs in row 2, [ch 1, sl st in 2nd ch of ch-3 sp, ch 1, 3 dc in next ch-3 sp on next motif, ch 1, 3 dc in next ch-1 sp, ch 1, 3 dc in next ch-3 sp] twice.

Motif 3A

Rep Motif 2A.

Motif 3B

Rep Motif 2B.

Motif 3C

Rep Motif 2C.

Working across incomplete motifs in row 3, ch 1, sl st in 2nd ch of ch-2 sp, ch 1, 3 dc in next ch-3 sp on next motif, ch 1, 3 dc in next ch-1 sp, ch 1, 3 dc in next ch-3 sp, ch 1, sl st in 2nd ch of ch-2 sp, ch 1, 3 dc in next ch-3 sp, ch 1, 3 dc in next ch-1 sp, ch 1, (3 dc, ch 3, 3 dc) in next ch-3 sp, ch 1, 3 dc in next ch-1 sp, ch 1, 3 dc in next ch-3 sp.

Working across incomplete motifs in column A, [ch 1, sl st in 2nd ch of ch-2 sp, ch 1, 3 dc in next ch-3 sp on next motif, ch 1, 3 dc in next ch-1 sp, ch 1, 3 dc in next ch-3 sp] twice, ch 1, sl st in 2nd ch of beg ch. Fasten off.

> **Note**
>
> The brim is worked sideways along the edge of the hat, alternating between rows of hdc-blo and sc-blo. For a folded-over brim, work double the amount of stitches stated for each folded-over row.

Jamie Hat

Refer to the instructions for the Jamie Motif at left for motifs referenced in these instructions; refer to Stitch Diagram B and the Construction Diagram on page 89 for assistance.

Motif 1

Work same as Motif 1A.

Motifs 2–5

Work same as Motif 1B.

Motif 6

Work same as Motif C.

Working across incomplete motifs in row 1, [ch 1, sl st in 2nd ch of ch-2 sp, ch 1, 3 dc in next ch-3 sp on next motif, ch 1, 3 dc in next ch-1 sp, ch 1, 3 dc in next ch-3 sp] 5 times.

Motif 7

Work same as Motif 2A.

Motifs 8–11

Work same as Motif 2B.

Motif 12

Work same as Motif 2C.

Working across incomplete motifs in row 2, [ch 1, sl st in 2nd ch of ch-3 sp, ch 1, 3 dc in next ch-3 sp on next motif, ch 1, 3 dc in next ch-1 sp, ch 1, 3 dc in next ch-3 sp] 5 times.

Motif 13

RND 1: Ch 22, sl st in 7th ch from hook to form ring, sl st in ea of next 3 chs (counts as dc), 2 dc in ring, [ch 3, 3 dc] 5 times in ring, ch 1, sl st to 2nd ch of beg ch (counts as ch-3).

RND 2: Sl st in ea of next 3 chs (counts as dc), 2 dc in same ch-3 sp, [ch 1, (3 dc, ch 3, 3 dc) in next ch-3 sp] 5 times, ch 1, 3 dc in next ch-3 sp, ch 1, sl st to 2nd ch of beg ch (counts as ch-3).

Note: On Rnd 3, Motif 13 (hexagon shaped with 6 sides labeled a–f on Stitch Diagram B) will join to the top edge of Motifs 7–12 as follows: 7/a, 8/b, 9/c, 10/d, 11/e, 12/f. At the end of Motif 13, continue along the incomplete edge of Motifs 7 and 1, while at the same time joining them to the side edge of Motifs 12 and 6, respectively.

RND 3: Sl st in ea of next 3 chs (counts as dc), 2 dc in same ch-3 sp, sl st in ch-1 sp on adjacent Motif 7, 3 dc in next ch-1 sp, sl st in next ch-1 sp on Motif 7, (3 dc, ch 1, sl st in ch-3 sp on adjacent motif, ch 1, 3 dc) in next ch-3 sp, sl st in ch-1 sp on Motif 8, 3 dc in next ch-1 sp, sl st in next ch-1 sp on Motif 8, (3 dc, ch 1, sl st in ch-3 sp on adjacent motif, ch 1, 3 dc) in next ch-3 sp, sl st in ch-1 sp on Motif 9, 3 dc in next ch-1 sp, sl st in next ch-1 sp on Motif 9, (3 dc, ch 1, sl st in ch-3 sp on adjacent motif, ch 1, 3 dc) in next ch-3 sp, sl st in ch-1 sp on Motif 10, 3 dc in next ch-1 sp, sl st in next ch-1 sp on Motif 10, (3 dc, ch 1, sl st in ch-3 sp on adjacent motif, ch 1, 3 dc) in next ch-3 sp, sl st in ch-1 sp on Motif 11, 3 dc in next ch-1 sp, sl st in next ch-1 sp on Motif 11, in next ch-3 sp (3 dc, ch 1, sl st in ch-3 sp on adjacent motif, ch 1, 3 dc), sl st in ch-1 sp on Motif 12, 3 dc in next ch-1 sp, sl st in next ch-1 sp on Motif 12, 3 dc in next ch-3 sp.

Working across incomplete side edge of Motif 7 (while joining to Motif 12) and Motif 1 (while joining to Motif 6), ch 1, sl st in 2nd ch of ch-2 sp on Motif 7 and ch-3 sp of Motif 12, ch 1, 3 dc in next ch-3 sp on Motif 7, sl st in next ch-1 sp on Motif 12, 3 dc in next ch-1 sp on Motif 7, sl st in next ch-1 sp on Motif 12, 3 dc in next ch-3 sp on Motif 7, ch 1, sl st in 2nd ch of ch-2 bet Motifs 7 and 1 and in junction bet Motifs 12 and 6, ch 1, 3 dc in next ch-3 sp on Motif 1, sl st in next ch-1 sp on Motif 6, 3 dc in next ch-1 sp on Motif 1, sl st in next ch-1 sp on Motif 6, 3 dc in next ch-3 sp on Motif 1, ch 1, sl st in 2nd ch of ch-3 sp on Motifs 6 and 1, ch 1, sl st to top of ch-3 at beg of rnd to join. Do not fasten off.

Hat Band

ROW 1: Ch 7, sc in 2nd ch from hook and in ea ch across, sl st in next ch-sp on edge of hat—6 sc.

ROW 2: Hdc-blo in ea st across, turn—6 hdc-blo.

ROW 3: Ch 1, sc-blo in ea st across, sk next st on edge of hat, sl st in next st on edge of hat, turn.

Rep Rows 2–3 until you work completely around the hat.

Working through both thicknesses, sl st in free loop of ea starting ch and blo of ea st on last row across to seam band. Fasten off. Weave in ends.

Wet block to finished measurements and let dry.

STITCH DIAGRAM B

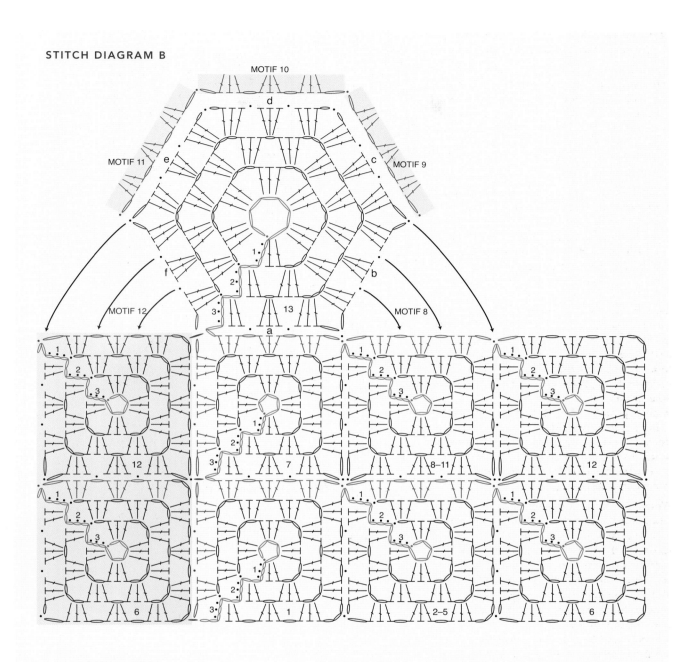

MOTIF 10

MOTIF 11 · e

MOTIF 9

MOTIF 12

MOTIF 8

CONSTRUCTION DIAGRAM

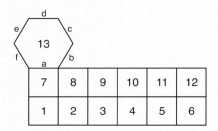

7	8	9	10	11	12
1	2	3	4	5	6

home décor

I think home décor pieces, such as cozy blankets, are the most wonderful gifts to give or receive in the realm of crochet. There are no sizing issues, and you know the recipient will use the gift when they are relaxing or to make their daily lives more enjoyable. The blanket, pillow, and trivets in this chapter utilize several construction styles to accentuate the versatility of seamless motifs. By mixing and matching the motifs and construction methods you will learn here, you can open up a whole world of possibilities for other projects.

moroccan tile
BLANKET

Moroccan tile-work is very inspiring to me and often re-minds me of crochet motifs. This is especially true when the corners of the tiles transform into another motif when lined up to other tiles with the identical design. This geometric detailing inspires many of my motifs, in-cluding the one used in this blanket. The center of the motif is quite simple, and the spade-shaped corners line up beautifully with the adjacent motifs to suggest a dif-ferent motif altogether. As an added bonus, the blanket requires no edging because the motifs naturally display a pretty scalloped detail.

YARN

Worsted weight (#4 Medium).

shown: Red Heart, Eco-Ways (70% acrylic/30% recycled polyester; 186 yd [170 m]/ 4 oz [113 g]): 8 balls of #3518 peacock.

HOOK

I/9 (5.5 mm) or size needed to obtain gauge.

NOTIONS

Tapestry needle for weaving in ends.

GAUGE

1 motif = 3¼" (8.5 cm) square after blocking.

FINISHED SIZE

39" wide x 52" long (99 x 132 cm).

moroccan tile *motif*

STITCH DIAGRAM A

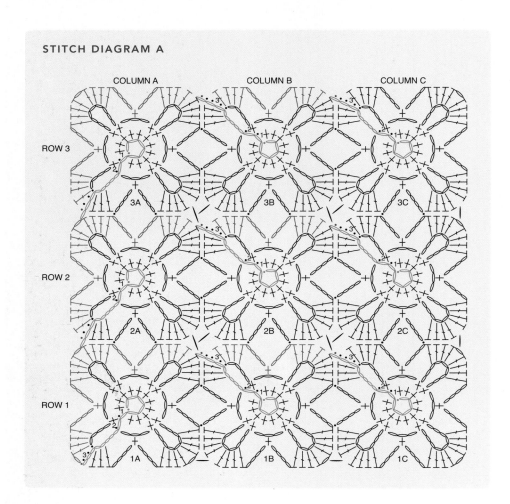

Refer to Stitch Diagram A above for assistance.

Motif 1A

RND 1: Ch 5 + 1 + 1 + 5 + 3 = 15, sl st in 5th ch from hook to form ring. Sl st in next ch (counts as sc), 11 sc in ring—2 sc.

RND 2: Sl st in next ch (counts as sc), *ch 3, sk next 2 sts, (sc, ch 9, sc) in next st. Rep from * twice. Ch 3, sk next 2 sts, sc in next st, ch 4, sl st in 5th ch of beg ch (counts as ch-9 loop).

RND 3: Sl st in ea of next 3 ch (counts as dc), 3 dc in same ch-9 sp, ch 4, sc in next ch-3 sp, ch 4, (4 dc, ch 1, 4 dc) in next ch-9 sp. Ch 4, sc in next ch-3 sp, ch 4, 4 dc in next ch-9 sp.

Motif 1B

RNDS 1–2: Rep Rnds 1–2 of Motif 1A.

RND 3: Sl st in ea of next 3 ch (counts as dc), 3 dc in same ch-9 sp, sl st in ch-4 sp on adjacent motif, *ch 4, sc in next ch-3 sp, ch 4, sl st in next ch-4 sp on adjacent motif, (4 dc, sl st in ch-1 sp on adjacent motif, 4 dc) in next ch-9 sp. Ch 4, sc in next ch-3 sp, ch 4, (4 dc, ch 1, 4 dc) in next ch-9 sp. Ch 4, sc in next ch-3 sp, ch 4, 4 dc in next ch-9 sp.

Motif 1C

RNDS 1–2: Rep Rnds 1–2 of Motif 1A.

RND 3: Sl st in ea of next 3 ch (counts as dc), 3 dc in same ch-9 sp, sl st in ch-4 sp on adjacent motif, *ch 4, sc in next ch-3 sp, ch 4, sl st in next ch-4 sp on adjacent motif, (4 dc, sl st in ch-1 sp on adjacent motif, 4 dc) in next ch-9 sp. *Ch 4, sc in next ch-3 sp, ch 4, (4 dc, ch 1, 4 dc) in next ch-9 sp. Rep from * once. Ch 4, sc in next ch-3 sp, ch 4, 4 dc in last ch-9 sp.

Working across incomplete motifs in row 1, *sl st in sp before next motif, 4 dc in next ch-9 sp, ch 4, sc in next ch-3 sp, ch 4, 4 dc in next ch-9 sp. Rep from * once.

Motif 2A

RNDS 1–2: Rep Rnds 1–2 of Motif 1A.

RND 3: Sl st in ea of next 3 ch (counts as dc), 3 dc in same ch-9 sp, sl st in ch-4 sp on adjacent motif (Motif 1A), ch 4, sc in next ch-3 sp, ch 4, sl st in next ch-4 sp on adjacent motif (Motif 1A), (4 dc, sl st in junction on adjacent motif, 4 dc) in next ch-9 sp. Ch 4, sc in next ch-3 sp, ch 4, 4 dc in next ch-9 sp.

Motif 2B

RNDS 1–2: Rep Rnds 1–2 of Motif 1A.

RND 3: Sl st in ea of next 3 ch (counts as dc), 3 dc in same ch-9 sp, sl st in ch-4 sp on adjacent motif (Motif 2A), ch 4, sc in next ch-3 sp, ch 4, sl st in next ch-4 sp on adjacent motif (Motif 2A), (4 dc, sl st in junction on adjacent motif, 4 dc) in next ch-9 sp. Sl st in ch-4 sp on adjacent motif (Motif 1B), ch 4, sc in next ch-3 sp, ch 4, sl st in next ch-4 sp on adjacent motif (Motif 1B), (4 dc, sl st in junction on adjacent motif, 4 dc) in next ch-9 sp. Ch 4, sc in next ch-3 sp, ch 4, 4 dc in next ch-9 sp.

Motif 2C

RNDS 1–2: Rep Rnds 1–2 of Motif 1A.

RND 3: Sl st in ea of next 3 ch (counts as dc), 3 dc in same ch-9 sp, sl st in ch-4 sp on adjacent motif (Motif 2B), *ch 4, sc in next ch-3 sp, ch 4, sl st in next ch-4 sp on adjacent motif (Motif 2B), (4 dc, sl st in junction on adjacent motif, 4 dc) in next ch-9 sp. Sl st in ch-4 sp on adjacent motif (Motif 1C), ch 4, sc in next ch-3 sp, ch 4, sl st in next ch-4 sp on adjacent motif (Motif 1C), (4 dc, sl st in ch-1 on adjacent motif, 4 dc) in next ch-9 sp, ch 4, sc in next ch-3 sp, ch 4, (4 dc, ch 1, 4 dc) in next ch-9 sp, ch 4, sc in next ch-3 sp, ch 4, 4 dc in next ch-9 sp.

Working across incomplete motifs in row 2, *sl st in sp before next motif, 4 dc in next ch-9 sp, ch 4, sc in next ch-3 sp, ch 4, 4 dc in next ch-9 sp. Rep from * once.

Motif 3A

Rep Motif 2A.

Motif 3B

Rep Motif 2B.

Motif 3C

Rep Motif 2C.

Working across incomplete motifs in row 3, sl st in sp before next motif, 4 dc in next ch-9 sp, ch 4, sc in next ch-3 sp, ch 4, 4 dc in next ch-9 sp. Sl st in sp before next motif, 4 dc in next ch-9 sp, ch 4, sc in next ch-3 sp, ch 4, (4 dc, ch 1, 4 dc) in next ch-9 sp, ch 4, sc in next ch-3 sp, ch 4, 4 dc in next ch-9 sp.

Working across side edge of incomplete motifs in column A, sl st in sp before next motif, 4 dc in next ch-9 sp, ch 4, sc in next ch-3 sp, ch 4, 4 dc in next ch-9 sp. Sl st in next sp before next motif, 4 dc in next ch-9 sp, ch 4, sc in next ch-3 sp, ch 4, 4 dc in next ch-9 sp, sl st to first ch at beg of Motif 1A to join. Fasten off.

Moroccan Tile Blanket

Refer to the instructions for the Moroccan Tile Motif on page 94 for motifs referenced in these instructions; refer to Stitch Diagram B below for assistance.

Motif 1

Work same as Motif 1A.

Motifs 2–15

Work same as Motif 1B.

Motif 16

Work same as Motif 1C.

Working across incomplete Motifs 15–1, *sl st in sp before next motif, 4 dc in next ch-9 sp, ch 4, sc in next ch-3 sp, ch 4, 4 dc in next ch-9 sp. Rep from * 14 times.

Motif 17

Work same as Motif 2A.

STITCH DIAGRAM B

Motif 18–31

Work same as Motif 2B.

Motif 32

Work same as Motif 2C.

Working across incomplete Motifs 31–17, *sl st in sp before next motif, 4 dc in next ch-9 sp, ch 4, sc in next ch-3 sp, ch 4, 4 dc in next ch-9 sp. Rep from * 14 times.

Motifs 33–192

Rep Motifs 17–32 ten times.

Working across incomplete Motifs 191–177, *sl st in sp before next motif, 4 dc in next ch-9 sp, ch 4, sc in next ch-3 sp, ch 4, 4 dc in next ch-9 sp. Rep from * 13 times. Sl st in ch-1 sp before next motif, 4 dc in next ch-9 sp, ch 4, sc in next ch-3 sp, ch 4, (4 dc, ch 1, 4 dc) in next ch-9 sp, ch 4, sc in next ch-3 sp, ch 4, 4 dc in next ch-9 sp.

Working along side edge of incomplete Motifs 161, 145, 129, 113, 97, 81, 65, 49, 33, 17, and 1, *sl st in sp before next motif, 4 dc in next ch-9 sp, ch 4, sc in next ch-3 sp, ch 4, 4 dc in next ch-9 sp. Rep from * 9 times. Sl st in sp before next motif, 4 dc in next ch-9 sp, ch 4, sc in next ch-3 sp, ch 4, 4 dc in next ch-9 sp, sl st to first ch at beg of Motif 1. Fasten off. Weave in ends.

Wet block to finished measurements and let dry.

flower
TRIVETS

These one-skein trivets are quick and easy, and they are the perfect complement to your dinner table setting. Not only will they protect your table from hot dishes, they'll also add color and panache to your mealtime spread. Each of the two samples feature a unique edging, giving you options to customize this project for gifts or for yourself. The sweet flower motif featured in the trivets evokes thoughts of springtime blooms and could also be used for a pretty throw to keep away the winter blues.

YARN

Worsted weight (#4 Medium).

shown: Lion Brand Yarn, Lion Cotton (100% pure cotton; 236 yd [212 m]/5 oz [140 g]): 123 sea spray (shown as option 1) and/or 145 orchid (shown as edging option 2), 1 ball per trivet.

HOOK

H/8 (5 mm) or size needed to obtain gauge.

NOTIONS

Tapestry needle for weaving in ends.

GAUGE

1 Motif = 2¾" (7 cm) in diameter.

FINISHED SIZE

12" x 12" (30.5 x 30.5 cm).

flower *motif*

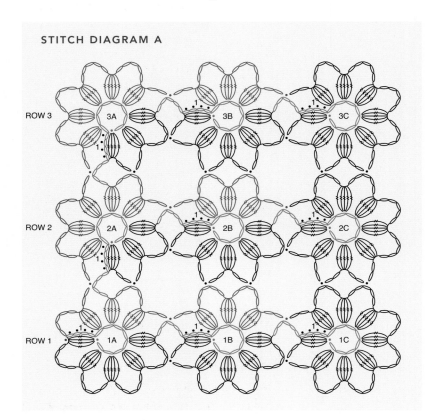

Special Stitches

Beg Popcorn Stitch (beg popcorn): Sl st in each of next 4 chs (counts as 1st tr), 4 tr in ring, drop loop from hook, insert hook from front to back in the top of the first tr of group (top of ch-4), pick up dropped loop and pull through loop on hook.

Popcorn Stitch (popcorn): 5 tr in same ring, drop loop from hook, insert hook from front to back in the top of the first tr of group, pick up dropped loop and pull through loop on hook.

Note

The instructions are for a 9-motif swatch (3 across × 3 down). But if you want to make a larger fabric, repeat the middle sections as suggested to modify your size.

Refer to Stitch Diagram B on page 102 for assistance.

Motif 1A

RND 1: Ch 8 + 4 = 12, sl st in 8th ch from hook to form ring. Beg popcorn in ring, [ch 5, popcorn in ring] 4 times.

Motif 1B

RND 1: Ch 17, sl st in 8th ch from hook to form ring. Beg popcorn in ring, ch 2, sl st in adjacent motif's (Motif 1A) ch-5 sp, ch 2, popcorn in ring, [ch 5, popcorn in ring] 3 times.

Motif 1C

RND 1: Ch 8 + 4 + 5 = 17, sl st in 8th ch from hook to form ring. Beg popcorn in ring, ch 2, sl st in ch-5 sp on adjacent motif (Motif 1B), ch 2, [popcorn, ch 5 in ring] 7 times, ch 2, sl st in 3rd ch of ch-5 sp bet motifs.

Working across incomplete motifs in row 1, ch 2, ([popcorn, ch 5] twice, popcorn, ch 2) in next ring (Motif 1B), sl st in 3rd ch of ch-5 sp bet motifs, ch 2, (popcorn, ch 5, popcorn) in next ring (Motif 1A).

Motif 2A

RND 1: Ch 17, sl st in 8th ch from hook to form ring. Beg popcorn in ring, ch 2, sl st in adjacent motif's (Motif 1A) ch-5 sp, ch 2, (popcorn, ch 5, popcorn) in ring.

Motif 2B

RND 1: Ch 17, sl st in 8th ch from hook to form ring. Beg popcorn in ring, ch 2, sl st in ch-5 sp on adjacent motif (Motif 2A), ch 2, popcorn in ring, *ch 2, sl st in ch-5 sp on adjacent motif (Motif 1B), ch 2, popcorn in ring. Rep from * once, ch 5, popcorn in ring.

Motif 2C

RND 1: Ch 17, sl st in 8th ch from hook to form ring. Beg popcorn in ring, ch 2, sl st in ch-5 sp on adjacent motif (Motif 2B) ch 2, popcorn in ring, *ch 2, sl st in ch-5 sp on adjacent motif (Motif 1C), ch 2, popcorn in ring. Rep from * once, [ch 5, popcorn in ring] 4 times, ch 2, sl st in 3rd ch of ch-5 sp bet motifs.

Working across incomplete motifs in row 2, ch 2, ([popcorn, ch 5] twice, popcorn, ch 2) in next ring (Motif 2B), sl st in 3rd ch of ch-5 sp bet motifs, ch 2, (popcorn, ch 5, popcorn) in next ring (Motif 2A).

Motif 3A

Rep Motif 2A.

Motif 3B

Rep Motif 2B.

Motif 3C

Rep Motif 2C.

Working across incomplete motifs in row 3, ch 2, ([popcorn, ch 5] twice, popcorn, ch 2) in next ring (Motif 3B), sl st in 3rd ch of ch-5 sp bet motifs, ch 2, ([popcorn, ch 5] 4 times, popcorn, ch 2) in next ring (Motif 3A).

Working across side edge of incomplete motifs in column A, sl st in 3rd ch of ch-5 sp bet motifs, ch 2, ([popcorn, ch 5] twice, popcorn, ch 2) in next ring (Motif 2A), ch 2, sl st in 3rd ch of ch-5 sp bet motifs, ch 2, popcorn in next ring (Motif 1A), ch 5, sl st in beg popcorn on Motif 1A to join. Fasten off.

Flower Trivets

Refer to the instructions for the Flower Motif on page 100 for motifs referenced in these instructions; refer to Stitch Diagram B on page 102 for assistance.

Motif 1

Work same as Motif 1A.

Motifs 2–3

Work same as Motif 1B.

Motif 4

Work same as Motif 1C.

Working across incomplete motifs in row 2, ch 2, *([popcorn, ch 5] twice, popcorn, ch 2) in next ring, sl st in 3rd ch of ch-5 sp bet motifs, ch 2. Rep from * once, (popcorn, ch 5, popcorn) in next ring.

Motif 5

Work same as Motif 2A.

Motifs 6–7

Work same as Motif 2B.

Motif 8

Work same as Motif 2C.

Working across incomplete motifs in row 2, ch 2, *([popcorn, ch 5] twice, popcorn, ch 2) in next ring, sl st in 3rd ch of ch-5 sp bet motifs, ch 2. Rep from * once, (popcorn, ch 5, popcorn) in next ring.

Special Stitches

Reverse Single Crochet (RSC): Working from left to right, insert hook into next st, yo, draw loop to front of work, yo and draw through both loops on hook.

Refer to Special Stitches on page 100 for other special stitches used in this pattern.

Motifs 9–16

Rep Motifs 5–8 twice.

Working across incomplete motifs in row 2, ch 2, *([popcorn, ch 5] twice, popcorn, ch 2) in next ring, sl st in 3rd ch of ch-5 sp bet motifs, ch 2. Rep from * once, ([popcorn, ch 5] 4 times, popcorn, ch 2) in next ring.

Working across side edge of incomplete motifs 13, 9, 5, 1, *sl st in 3rd ch of ch-5 sp bet motifs, ch 2, ([popcorn, ch 5] twice, popcorn, ch 2) in next ring. Rep from * once, sl st in 3rd ch of ch-5 sp bet motifs, ch 2, popcorn in next ring, ch 5, sl st in first ch of beg ch-4 to join. Do not fasten off.

Edging 1 *(option 1)*

ROW 1: Sl st in next ch-5 sp, ch 3 (counts as dc), 6 more dc in same sp, *7 dc in next ch-5 sp. Rep from * around, skipping all ch-2 sps. Join with sl st in top of ch-3 at beg of rnd. Fasten off.

Edging 2 *(option 2)*

ROW 1: Ch 1, working from left to right, 5 RSC sts in ea ch-5 sp and 2 RSC in ea ch-2 sp around. Join with sl st in first st at beg of rnd. Fasten off. Weave in ends.

Wet block, pin to finished measurements, and let dry.

STITCH DIAGRAM B

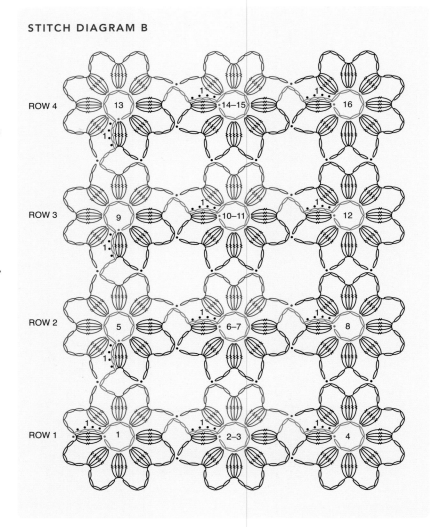

EDGING OPTION 1

EDGING OPTION 2

raspberry
PILLOW

This bright, fun pillow would be a great accent for a sofa or bed. I just love the juxtaposition of the circular motif with corners because when the motif corners are joined, they look like a separate motif from the circular centers. Even though the motifs have several rounds, they are very simple and can be worked up quickly to make this over-sized pillow. Based on the gauge of your squares, you could easily convert this to any pillow size, including a body pillow or floor cushion.

YARN

Worsted weight (#4 Medium).

shown: Red Heart, Super Saver Economy (100% acrylic; 364 yd [333 m]/7 oz [198 g]): 2 balls of #0905 magenta.

HOOK

H/8 (5 mm) or size needed to obtain gauge.

NOTIONS

Tapestry needle for weaving in ends; 26" (66 cm) square pillow form in desired color (to complement yarn color).

GAUGE

1 motif = 6½" (16.5 cm) square.

FINISHED SIZE

26" x 52" (66 x 132 cm) flat fabric (8 motifs wide x 4 motifs tall); 26" (66 cm) square finished pillow cover.

raspberry *motif*

STITCH DIAGRAM A

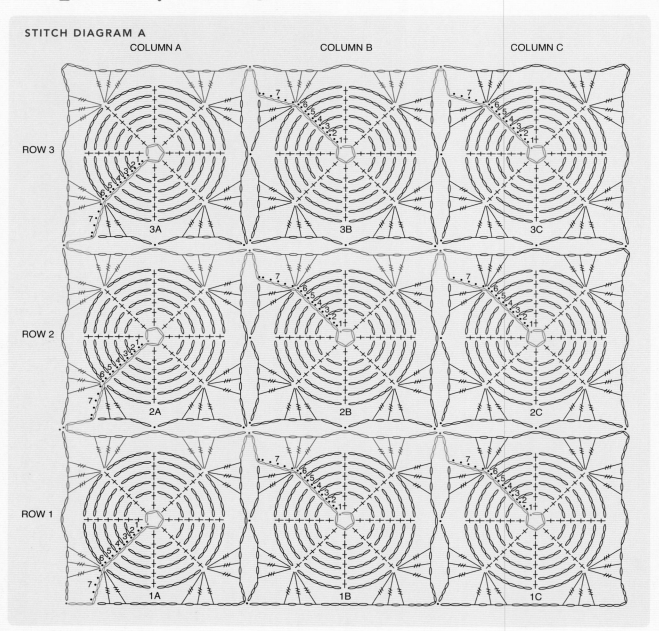

Refer to stitch diagram A above for assistance.

Motif 1A

RND 1: Ch 5 + 6 + 5 + 3 = 19, sl st in 5th ch from hook to join ring. Sl st in next ch (counts as sc), 7 sc in ring, sl st in first st at beg of rnd—8 sc.

RND 2: Sl st in next ch (counts as sc), *ch 2, sc in next sc. Rep from * around, ch 2, sl st in first st at beg of rnd—8 ch-2 sps.

RND 3: Sl st in next ch (counts as sc), *ch 3, sc in next sc. Rep from * around, ch 3, sl st in first st at beg of rnd—8 ch-3 sps.

RND 4: Sl st in next ch (counts as sc), *ch 4, sc in next sc. Rep from * around, ch 4, sl st in first st at beg of rnd—8 ch-4 sps.

RND 5: Sl st in next ch (counts as sc), *ch 5, sc in next sc. Rep from * around, ch 5, sl st in first st at beg of rnd—8 ch-5 sps.

RND 6: Sl st in next ch (counts as sc), *ch 6, sc in next sc. Rep from * around, ch 6, sl st in first st at beg of rnd—8 ch-6 sps.

RND 7: Sl st in ea of next 5 chs (counts as dtr), ch 1, (dtr, ch 1, dtr) in same st, *ch 5, sk next sc, (dtr, ch 1, dtr, ch 1, dtr, ch 7, dtr, ch 1, dtr, ch 1, dtr) in next sc. Ch 5, sk next sc, (dtr, ch 1, dtr, ch 1, dtr) in next sc.

Motif 1B

RND 1: Ch 5 + 6 + 5 + 7 = 23, sl st in 5th ch from hook to join ring. Sl st in next ch (counts as sc), 7 sc in ring, sl st in first st at beg of rnd—8 sc.

RNDS 2–6: Rep Rnds 2–6 of Motif 1A.

RND 7: Sl st in ea of next 5 beg chs (counts as dtr), ch 1, (dtr, ch 1, dtr) in same st, ch 2, sl st in ch-5 sp on adjacent motif, ch 2, sk next sc, (dtr, ch 1, dtr, ch 1, dtr, ch 3, sl st in 4th ch of ch-7 sp on adjacent motif, ch 3, dtr, ch 1, dtr, ch 1, dtr) in next sc. Ch 5, sk next sc, (dtr, ch 1, dtr, ch 1, dtr, ch 7, dtr, ch 1, dtr, ch 1, dtr) in next sc. Ch 5, sk next sc, (dtr, ch 1, dtr, ch 1, dtr) in next sc.

Motif 1C

RNDS 1–6: Rep Rnds 1–6 of Motif 1B.

RND 7: Sl st in ea of next 5 beg chs (counts as dtr), ch 1, (dtr, ch 1, dtr) in same st, ch 2, sl st in ch-5 sp on adjacent motif, ch 2, sk next sc, (dtr, ch 1, dtr, ch 1, dtr, ch 3, sl st in 4th ch of ch-7 sp on adjacent motif, ch 3, dtr, ch 1, dtr, ch 1, dtr) in next sc. *Ch 5, sk next sc, (dtr, ch 1, dtr, ch 1, dtr, ch 7, dtr, ch 1, dtr, ch 1, dtr) in next sc. Rep from * once. Ch 5, sk next sc, (dtr, ch 1, dtr, ch 1, dtr) in next sc.

Working across incomplete motifs in row 1, *ch 3, sl st in 4th ch of ch-7 sp, ch 3, (dtr, ch 1, dtr, ch 1, dtr) in next sc, ch 5, sk next sc, (dtr, ch 1, dtr, ch 1, dtr) in next sc. Rep from * once.

Motif 2A

RNDS 1–6: Rep Rnds 1–6 of Motif 1B.

RND 7: Sl st in ea of next 5 beg chs (counts as dtr), ch 1, (dtr, ch 1, dtr) in same st, ch 2, sl st in ch-5 sp on adjacent motif, ch 2, sk next sc, (dtr, ch 1, dtr, ch 1, dtr, ch 3, sl st in 4th ch of ch-7 sp on adjacent motif, ch 3, dtr, ch 1, dtr, ch 1, dtr) in next sc. Ch 5, sk next sc, (dtr, ch 1, dtr, ch 1, dtr) in next sc.

Motif 2B

RNDS 1–6: Rep Rnds 1–6 of Motif 1B.

RND 7: Sl st in ea of next 5 beg chs (counts as dtr), ch 1, (dtr, ch 1, dtr) in same st, *ch 2, sl st in ch-5 sp on adjacent motif, ch 2, sk next sc, (dtr, ch 1, dtr, ch 1, dtr, ch 3, sl st in 4th ch of ch-7 sp on adjacent motif, ch 3, dtr, ch 1, dtr, ch 1, dtr) in next sc. Rep from * once, ch 5, sk next sc, (dtr, ch 1, dtr, ch 1, dtr) in next sc.

Motif 2C

RNDS 1–6: Rep Rnds 1–6 of Motif 1B.

RND 7: Sl st in ea of next 5 beg chs (counts as dtr), ch 1, (dtr, ch 1, dtr) in same st, *ch 2, sl st in ch-5 sp on adjacent motif, ch 2, sk next sc, (dtr, ch 1, dtr, ch 1, dtr, ch 3, sl st in 4th ch of ch-7 sp on adjacent motif, ch 3, dtr, ch 1, dtr, ch 1, dtr) in next sc. Rep from * once, ch 5, sk next sc, (dtr, ch 1, dtr, ch 1, dtr, ch 7, dtr, ch 1, dtr, ch 1, dtr) in next sc. Ch 5, sk next sc, (dtr, ch 1, dtr, ch 1, dtr) in next sc.

Working across incomplete motifs in row 2, *ch 3, sl st in 4th ch of ch-7 sp, ch 3, (dtr, ch 1, dtr, ch 1, dtr) in next sc, ch 5, sk next sc, in next sc (dtr, ch 1, dtr, ch 1, dtr). Rep from * once.

Motif 3A

Rep Motif 2A.

Motif 3B

Rep Motif 2B.

Motif 3C

Rep Motif 2C.

Working across incomplete motifs in row 3, *ch 3, sl st in 4th ch of ch-7 sp, ch 3, (dtr, ch 1, dtr, ch 1, dtr) in next sc, ch 5, sk next sc, (dtr, ch 1, dtr, ch 1, dtr) in next sc. Rep from * once, ch 7, (dtr, ch 1, dtr, ch 1, dtr) in same st, ch 5, sk next sc, (dtr, ch 1, dtr, ch 1, dtr) in next sc.

Working across side edge of incomplete motifs in column A, *ch 3, sl st in 4th ch of ch-7 sp, ch 3, (dtr, ch 1, dtr, ch 1, dtr) in next sc, ch 5, sk next sc, (dtr, ch 1, dtr, ch 1, dtr) in next sc. Rep from * once, ch 3, sl st to first ch of beg ch on Motif 1A to join. Fasten off.

Raspberry Pillow

Pillow cover is made according to instructions for the Raspberry Motif on page 106, working a rectangle of 8 motifs wide by 4 motifs deep.

Refer to Stitch Diagram B at right for assistance.

Motif 1

Work same as Motif 1A.

Motifs 2–7

Work same as Motif 1B.

Motif 8

Work same as Motif 1C.

Working across incomplete motifs in row 1, *ch 3, sl st in 4th ch of ch-7 sp, ch 3, (dtr, ch 1, dtr, ch 1, dtr) in next sc, ch 5, sk next sc, (dtr, ch 1, dtr, ch 1, dtr) in next sc. Rep from * 6 times.

Motif 9

Work same as Motif 2A.

Motifs 10–15

Work same as Motif 2B

Motif 16

Work same as Motif 2C

Working across incomplete motifs in row 2, *ch 3, sl st in 4th ch of ch-7 sp, ch 3, (dtr, ch 1, dtr, ch 1, dtr) in next sc, ch 5, sk next sc, (dtr, ch 1, dtr, ch 1, dtr) in next sc. Rep from * 6 times.

Motifs 17–32

Rep Motifs 9–16.

Working across incomplete motifs in row 3, *ch 3, sl st in 4th ch of ch-7 sp, ch 3, (dtr, ch 1, dtr, ch 1, dtr) in next sc, ch 5, sk next sc, (dtr, ch 1, dtr, ch 1, dtr) in next sc. Rep from * 6 times.

Motifs 25-32

Rep Motifs 9–16.

Working across incomplete motifs in row 4, *ch 3, sl st in 4th ch of ch-7 sp, ch 3, (dtr, ch 1, dtr, ch 1, dtr) in next sc, ch 5, sk next sc, (dtr, ch 1, dtr, ch 1, dtr) in next sc. Rep from * 6 times,

ch 7, (dtr, ch 1, dtr, ch 1, dtr) in same st, ch 5, sk next sc, (dtr, ch 1, dtr, ch 1, dtr) in next sc.

Working along side edge of incomplete motifs in column A, *ch 3, sl st in 4th ch of ch-7 sp, ch 3, (dtr, ch 1, dtr, ch 1, dtr) in next sc, ch 5, sk next sc, (dtr, ch 1, dtr, ch 1, dtr) in next sc. Rep from * twice, ch 3, sl st to first ch of beg ch-4 to join (counts as ch-7 sp). Do not fasten off.

Edging

ROW 1: Working across long edge of piece, ch 3 (counts as dc), 2 dc in same sp, *1 dc in each of next (st, ch, st, ch, st), 5 dc in next ch-5 sp, 1 dc in each of next (st, ch, st, ch, st), 3 dc in each of next 2 ch-sps*. Rep from * to 6 times. 1 dc in each of next (st, ch, st, ch, st), 5 dc in next ch-5 sp, 1 dc in each of next (st, ch, st, ch, st), 12 dc in next ch-7 sp. Rep from * to * 3 times, 12 dc in next ch-7 sp, 1 dc in each of next (st, ch, st, ch, st), 5 dc in next ch-5 sp, 1 dc in each of next (st, ch, st, ch, st), 12 dc in next ch-7 sp. Rep from * to * 7 times. 1 dc in each of next (st, ch, st, ch, st), 5 dc in next ch-5 sp, 1 dc in each of next (st, ch, st, ch, st), 3 dc in next ch-sp. Fasten off.

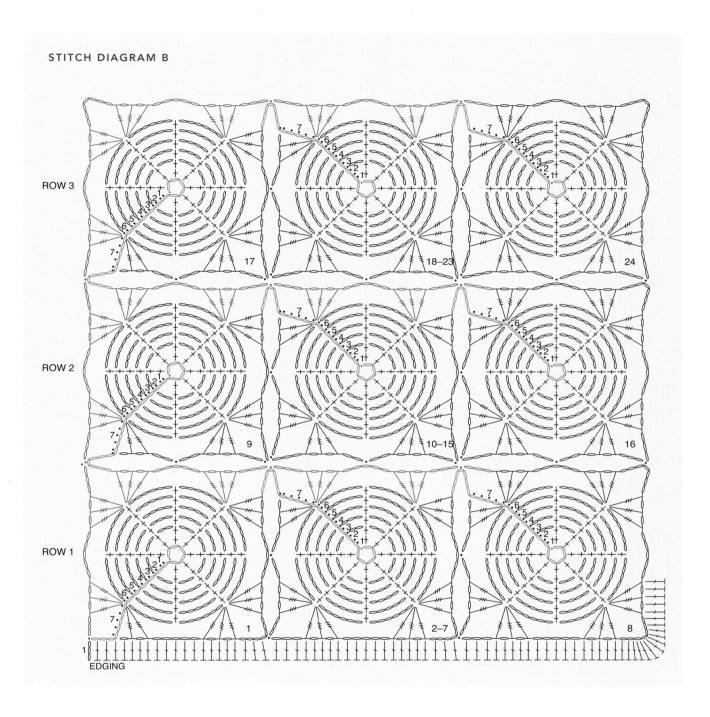

Assembly

Fold fabric in half lengthwise so you have a doubled fabric of 4 squares x 4 squares with right sides facing. Join yarn in 84th dc to the right of corner, in dc at corner of Motif 4 adjacent to fold. Working through both thicknesses, matching sts, sl st in each st across 3 sides, inserting your pillow form before closing up the entire pillow cover. Fasten off. Weave in ends.

babies and kids

I learned to crochet by making baby items while pregnant with my son. It is exciting for me to debut my first baby and kid collection to pay homage to my crochet roots. In this chapter, you'll find something for everyone. The Buttercup Blanket (page 114) is the girliest of girly blankets with tons of textured flowers! The Shark Hunter Blanket (page 120), named for my son (whose nickname is the shark hunter), features a fantastic double-layer shark-tooth edging that kids will love. There is also a Shark Hunter Hat (page 126) to match the blanket and even a Starfish Blanket (page 130), which features a very cool starfish motif.

buttercup
BLANKET

I love this three-dimensional flower motif, and I think it creates the perfect texture to wrap up and snuggle with your little bundle of joy. The two-tiered flowers have a whimsical, feminine appeal for your favorite girly-girl. The motifs also serve to make a surprisingly dense fabric that is warm and cozy. The simple edging creates a nice contrast with the body of the blanket and provides an attractive, crisp finish.

YARN

DK weight (#3 Light).

shown: Naturally Caron, Spa (25% rayon from bamboo/ 75% microdenier acrylic; 251 yd [230 m]/ 3 oz [85 g]): 7 balls of #0002 coral lipstick (MC); 1 ball each of #0007 naturally (A); #0003 soft sunshine (B); and #0001 rose bisque (C).

Note: If making blanket with one color only, 8 balls of MC are required.

HOOK

H/8 (5 mm) or size needed to obtain gauge.

NOTIONS

Tapestry needle for weaving in ends.

GAUGE

1 motif = 2½" (6.5 cm) square after blocking.

FINISHED SIZE

30" x 35" (76 x 91.5 cm).

buttercup *motif*

STITCH DIAGRAM A

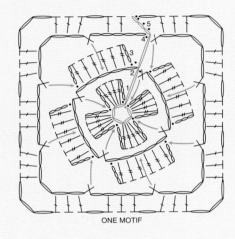

ONE MOTIF

STITCH DIAGRAM B

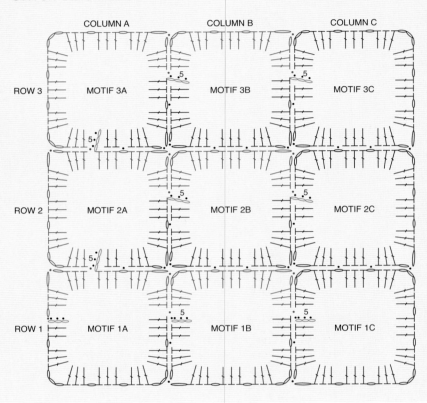

Refer to Stitch Diagram A above for assistance.

Note: The instructions are for a 9-motif swatch (3 rows × 3 columns). But if you want to make a larger fabric, repeat the middle sections as suggested to modify your size.

Motif 1A

RND 1: Ch 5 + 1 + 1 + 3 = 10, sl st in 5th ch from hook to form ring. Sl st in ring, [ch 3, 4 tr, ch 3, sl st] 4 times in ring.

RND 2: Sl st in next ch of beg ch, *ch 5, working behind petals of Rnd 1, sc in next sl st. Rep from * 3 times.

RND 3: *(Sl st, ch 3, 6 tr, ch 3, sl st) in next ch-5 sp. Rep from * 3 times, sl st to first sl st to join.

RND 4: Sl st in next ch of beg ch (counts as sc), *ch 5, working behind petals of Rnd 3, sc in next ch-5 sp bet 3rd and 4th tr in Rnd 2. Ch 5, sc in next sl st. Rep from * 3 times.

RND 5: Sl st into next ch-5 sp, sl st in ea of last 3 chs of beg ch (counts as dc), 2 dc in next ch-5 sp, *ch 1, (3 dc, ch 3, 3 dc) in next ch-5 sp, ch 1, 3 dc in next ch-5 sp, rep from * once.

Motif 1B

RNDS 1–4: Rep Rnds 1–4 of Motif 1A.

RND 5: Sl st in ea of last 3 chs of beg ch (counts as dc), 2 dc in next ch-5 sp, sl st in ch-1 sp on adjacent motif (Motif 1A),*(3 dc, ch 1, sl st in ch-3 sp on adjacent motif, ch 1, 3 dc) in next ch-5 sp, ch 1, 3 dc in next ch-5 sp, ch 1, (3 dc, ch 3, 3 dc) in next ch-5 sp, ch 1, 3 dc in next ch-5 sp.

Motif 1C

RNDS 1–4: Rep Rnds 1–4 of Motif 1A.

RND 5: Sl st in ea of last 3 chs of beg ch (counts as dc), 2 dc in next ch-5 sp, sl st in ch-1 sp on adjacent motif (Motif 2A), (3 dc, ch 1, sl st in ch-3 sp on adjacent motif, ch 1, 3 dc) in next ch-5 sp, *ch 1, 3 dc in next ch-5 sp, ch 1, (3 dc, ch 3, 3 dc) in next ch-5 sp. Rep from * twice.

Working across incomplete motifs in row 1, sl st in sp bet current and adjacent motifs, (3 dc, ch 1, sl st in ch-3 sp of adjacent Motif 1C, ch 1, 3 dc) in next ch-5 sp, ch 1, 3 dc in next ch-5 sp, ch 1, (3 dc, ch 3, 3 dc) in next ch-5 sp, sl st in sp bet current and adjacent motifs, working in next motif (Motif 1A) (3 dc, ch 1, sl st in ch-3 sp of adjacent Motif 1B, ch 1, 3 dc) in next ch-5 sp, ch 1, 3 dc in next ch-5 sp.

Motif 2A

RNDS 1–4: Rep Rnds 1–4 of Motif 1A.

RND 5: Sl st in ea of last 3 chs of beg ch (counts as dc), 2 dc in next ch-5 sp, sl st in ch-1 sp on adjacent motif (Motif 1A), (3 dc, ch 1, sl st in ch-3 sp on adjacent motif, ch 1, 3 dc) in next ch-5 sp, sl st in ch-1 sp on adjacent motif, ch 1, 3 dc in next ch-5 sp.

Motif 2B

RNDS 1–4: Rep Rnds 1–4 of Motif 1A.

RND 5: Sl st in ea of last 3 chs of beg ch (counts as dc), 2 dc in next ch-5 sp, sl st in ch-1 sp on adjacent motif (Motif 1B), (3 dc, ch 1, sl st in ch-3 sp on adjacent motif, ch 1, 3 dc) in next ch-5 sp, sl st in ch-1 sp on adjacent motif (Motif 2A), 3 dc in next ch-5 sp, sl st in ch-1 sp on adjacent motif, (3 dc, ch 1, sl st in ch-3 sp on adjacent motif, ch 1, 3 dc) in next ch-5 sp, ch 1, 3 dc in next ch-5 sp.

Motif 2C

RNDS 1–4: Rep Rnds 1–4 of Motif 1A.

RND 5: Sl st in ea of last 3 chs of beg ch (counts as dc), 2 dc in next ch-5 sp, sl st in ch-1 sp on adjacent motif (Motif 2B), (3 dc, ch 1, sl st in ch-3 sp on adjacent motif, ch 1, 3 dc) in next ch-5 sp, sl st in ch-1 sp on adjacent motif (Motif 2B), 3 dc in next ch-5 sp, sl st in ch-1 sp on adjacent motif, (3 dc, ch 1, sl st in ch-3 sp on adjacent motif, ch 1, 3 dc) in next ch-5 sp, ch 1, *3 dc in next ch-5 sp, (3 dc, ch 3, 3 dc) in next ch-5 sp. Rep from * once.

Working across incomplete motifs in row 2, sl st in sp bet current and adjacent motifs, (3 dc, ch 1, sl st in ch-3 sp of adjacent motif, ch 1, 3 dc) in next ch-5 sp, ch 1, 3 dc in next ch-5 sp, (3 dc, ch 3, 3 dc) in next ch-5 sp, sl st in sp bet cur-

rent and next motif, (3 dc, ch 1, sl st in ch-3 sp of adjacent motif, ch 1, 3 dc) in next ch-5 sp, ch 1, 3 dc in next ch-5 sp.

Motif 3A

Rep Motif 2A.

Motif 3B

Rep Motif 1B.

Motif 3C

Rep Motif 2C.

Working across incomplete motifs in row 3, sl st in sp bet current and next motif, (3 dc, ch 1, sl st in ch-3 sp of adjacent motif, ch 1, 3 dc) in next ch-5 sp, ch 1, 3 dc in next ch-5 sp, (3 dc, ch 3, 3 dc) in next ch-5 sp.

Working across incomplete motifs in Column A, *sl st in sp bet current and next motif, (3 dc, ch 1, sl st in ch-3 sp of adjacent motif, ch 1, 3 dc) in next ch-5 sp, ch 1, 3 dc in next ch-5 sp, (3 dc, ch 3, 3 dc) in next ch-5 sp * once, ch 1, 3 dc in next ch-5 sp, ch 1, (3 dc, ch 3, 3 dc) in next ch-5 sp. Rep from * to * once. Sl st in sp bet current and next motif, (3 dc, ch 1, sl st in ch-3 sp of adjacent motif, ch 1, 3 dc) in next ch-5 sp, ch 1, sl st in first ch of beg ch-3 on Motif 1A.

Fasten off. Weave in loose ends.

Buttercup Baby Blanket

Refer to the instructions for the Buttercup Motif on page 116 for motifs referenced in these instructions; refer to Stitch Diagram C at right for assistance.

Motif 1

Work same as Motif 1A.

Motifs 2–12

Work same as Motif 1B.

Motif 13

Work same as Motif 1C.

Completion Row

Working across incomplete motifs in row 1, *sl st in sp bet current and adjacent motifs, (3 dc, ch 1, sl st in ch-3 sp of adjacent motif, ch 1, 3 dc) in next ch-5 sp, ch 1, 3 dc in next ch-5 sp, ch 1, (3 dc, ch 3, 3 dc) in next ch-5 sp. Rep from * 10 times, sl st in sp bet current and adjacent motifs, working in next motif (3 dc, ch 1, sl st in ch-3 sp of adjacent motif, ch 1, 3 dc) in next ch-5 sp, ch 1, 3 dc in next ch-5 sp.

Motif 14

Work same as Motif 2A.

Motifs 15–25

Work same as Motif 2B.

Motif 26

Work same as Motif 2C.

Completion Row

Working across incomplete motifs in row 2, *sl st in sp bet current and adjacent motifs, (3 dc, ch 1, sl st in ch-3 sp of adjacent motif ch 1, 3 dc) in next ch-5 sp, ch 1, 3 dc in next ch-5 sp, ch 1, (3 dc, ch 3, 3 dc) in next ch-5 sp. Rep from * 10 times, sl st in sp bet current and adjacent motifs, working in next motif (3 dc, ch 1, sl st in ch-3 sp of adjacent motif, ch 1, 3 dc) in next ch-5 sp, ch 1, 3 dc in next ch-5 sp.

Motifs 27–143

Rep Motifs 14–26 nine times.

Completion Row

Working across incomplete motifs in last row, *sl st in sp bet current and next motif, (3 dc, ch 1, sl st in ch-3 sp of adjacent motif, ch 1, 3 dc) in next ch-5 sp, ch 1, 3 dc in next ch-5 sp, (3 dc, ch 3, 3 dc) in next ch-5 sp*. Rep from * to * 10 times, ch 1, 3 dc in next ch-5 sp, ch 1, (3 dc, ch 3, 3 dc) in next ch-5 sp. Rep from * to * 8 times. Sl st in sp bet current and next motif, (3 dc, ch 1, sl st in ch-3 sp of adjacent motif, ch 1, 3 dc) in next ch-5 sp, ch 1, sl st in first ch of beg ch-3 on Motif 1. Do not fasten off.

Edging

Note: If you are making the blanket in one color, follow Rnds 1–3 of Edging as written. If you are making the blanket with a multicolored edging, work Rnd 1 with A, Rnd 2 with B, and Rnd 3 with C. Fasten off the yarn after each rnd and join new color with sl st in first ch-1 sp.

RND 1: Sl st in next 2 dc, sl st in next ch-1 sp, ch 3 (counts as dc), 2 dc in same sp, ch 1, **(3 dc, ch 3, 3 dc) in next corner ch-3 sp, (3 dc, ch 1) in ea of next 2 ch-1 sps, *3 dc in sp bet motifs, ch 1, (3 dc, ch 1) in ea of next 2 ch-1 sps. Rep from * across to next ch-3 corner. Rep from ** around, join with sl st to top of beg ch-3–4 ch-3 corners.

RNDS 2–3: Sl st in next 2 dc, sl st in next ch-1 sp, ch 3 (counts as dc), 2 dc in same sp, ch 1, **(3 dc, ch 3, 3 dc) in next corner ch-3 sp, (3 dc, ch 1) in ea ch-1 sp across to next ch-3 corner. Rep from ** around, join with sl st to top of beg ch-3–4 ch-3 corners. Fasten off. Weave in ends.

Block to finished measurements and let dry.

Note: Due to the durable nature of the fiber in this yarn, the washing machine can be used for wet blocking.

STITCH DIAGRAM C

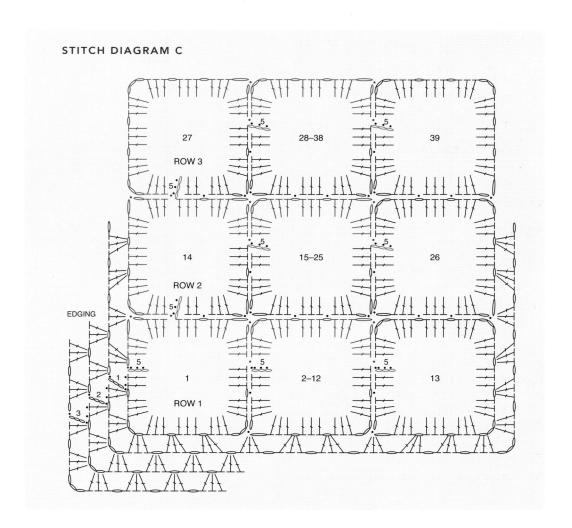

shark hunter
BLANKET

This blanket is dedicated to all the shark hunters out there. What little boy wouldn't love to have a blanket with a multilayered shark jaw for the border? The blanket tiles are easy to crochet and make a soothing, dense fabric. The edging is worked twice, once in the front loops of the blanket's border and once in the back loops, with the two rows of toothy edging offset by half a repeat.

YARN

Worsted weight (#4 Medium).

shown: Caron, Simply Soft (100% acrylic; 315 yd [288 m]/6 oz [170 g]): 4 skeins of # 9711 dark country blue (MC); 1 skein of #9701 white (CC).

HOOK

H/8 (5 mm) or size needed to obtain gauge.

NOTIONS

Tapestry needle for weaving in ends; straight pins for blocking.

GAUGE

1 motif = 5½" (14 cm) square.

FINISHED SIZE

38" (96.5 cm) square.

shark hunter *motif*

STITCH DIAGRAM A

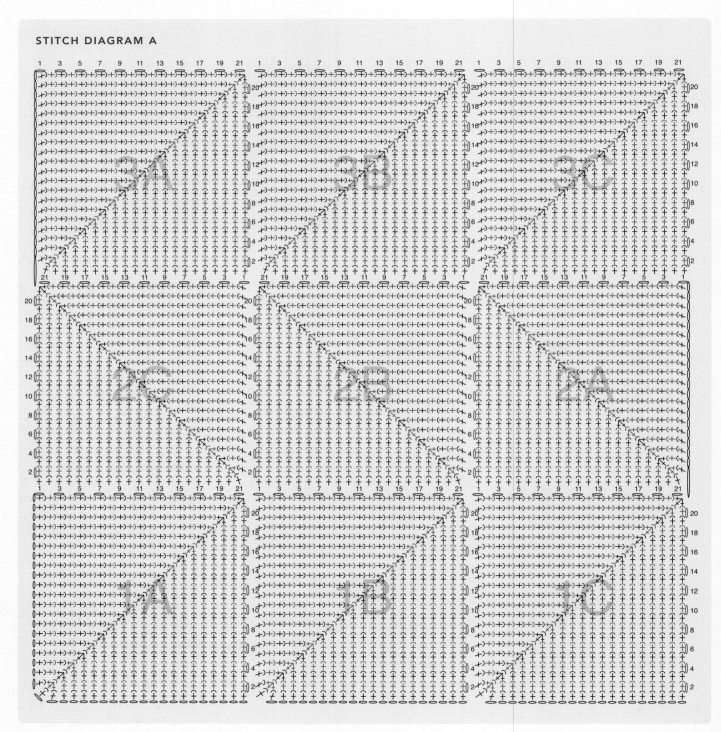

Refer to Stitch Diagram A at left for assistance.

Motif 1A

ROW 1: Work 41 fsc.

ROW 2: Ch 1, *sc-blo in ea of next 19 sts*, sc3tog-blo, rep from * to * once, turn—39 sts.

ROW 3: Ch 1, *sc-blo in ea of next 18 sts*, sc3tog-blo, rep from * to * once, turn—37 sts.

ROW 4: Ch 1, *sc-blo in ea of next 17 sts*, sc3tog-blo, rep from * to * once, turn—35 sts.

ROWS 5–20: Cont in est patt until 3 sts rem.

ROW 21 (LAST ROW): Ch 1, sc3tog-blo.

Motif 1B

ROW 1: Ch 1, work 20 sc evenly along ends of rows on previous square, work 21 fsc—41 sts.

ROWS 2–21: Rep Rows 2–21 of Motif 1A.

Motif 1C

Rep Motif 1B.

Motif 2A

ROW 1: Loosely ch 21, sc in 2nd ch from hook and in ea ch across, work 20 sc evenly along ends of rows of previous square—41 sts.

ROWS 2–21: Rep Rows 2–21 of Motif 1A.

Motif 2B

ROW 1: Ch 1, work 20 sc evenly along ends of rows on previous square, work 21 sc spaced evenly across Motif 1B—41 sts.

ROWS 2–21: Rep Rows 2–21 of Motif 1A.

Motif 2C

Rep Motif 2B.

Motif 3A

Rep Motif 2A.

Motif 3B

Rep Motif 2B.

Motif 3C

Rep Motif 2B.

Fasten off.

Shark Hunter Blanket

Refer to Stitch Diagram B on page 125 for assistance. Shark Hunter Motif instructions are at left.

Motif 1

ROW 1: Work 41 fsc.

ROW 2: Ch 1, *sc-blo in ea of next 19 sts*, sc3tog-blo, rep from * to * once, turn—39 sts.

ROW 3: Ch 1, *sc-blo in ea of next 18 sts*, sc3tog-blo, rep from * to * once, turn—37 sts.

ROW 4: Ch 1, *sc-blo in ea of next 17 sts*, sc3tog-blo, rep from * to * once, turn—35 sts.

ROWS 5–20: Cont in est patt until 3 sts rem.

ROW 21 (LAST ROW): Ch 1, sc3tog-blo. Do not fasten off.

Motif 2

ROW 1: Ch 1, work 20 sc evenly along ends of rows on previous square, work 21 fsc—41 sts.

ROWS 2–21: Rep Rows 2–21 of Motif 1.

Motifs 3–6

Rep Motif 2.

Motif 7

ROW 1: Loosely ch 21, sc in 2nd ch from hook and in ea ch across, work 20 sc evenly along ends of rows of previous square—41 sts.

Rows 2–22: Rep Rows 2–22 of Motif 1.

Motif 8

ROW 1: Ch 1, work 20 sc evenly along ends of rows on previous square, work 21 sc evenly spaced across next square in row 1, turn—41 sts.

Motifs 9–12

Rep Motif 8.

Motifs 13–18

Rep Motifs 7–12.

> **Note**
>
> Use MC for all motifs. CC will be used for Edging.

Motifs 19–24

Rep Motifs 7–12.

Motifs 25–30

Rep Motifs 7–12.

Motifs 31–36

Rep Motifs 7–12.

Do not fasten off.

Edging

RND 1: With MC, work 1 rnd of dc around entire perimeter of blanket, working 20 dc evenly across ea square, and 5 dc in ea of the 4 blanket corners—50 dc.

Fasten off.

RND 2A: With CC, join with sl st to back loop of any st. Ch 1, sc-blo in ea st around, sl st to join to first st at beg of rnd.

Note: Edging is worked twice, once in back loop (rnds marked A) and once in front loop (rnds marked B) of Rnd 1 of Edging.

RND 3A: *Ch 7, sc in 2nd ch from hook, hdc in next ch, dc in next ch, tr in next ch, dtr in ea of next 2 chs, sk next 4 sts on Rnd 2A, sl st in next st on Rnd 2A. Rep from * around. Fasten off.

RND 2B: With CC, sk front loop of st joined at beg of Rnd 2A and sk next 2 front loops. Join with sl st in front loop of next st on Rnd 1. Ch 1, sc-flo in ea st around, sl st to join first st at beg of rnd.

Note: The location of the beginning of Rnd 2B is changed from Rnd 2A so the shark teeth are offset to look more like the layers of teeth on a real shark jaw!

RND 3B: Rep Rnd 3A.

Fasten off.

Wet block to finished measurements, pinning teeth to dry flat. Weave in ends.

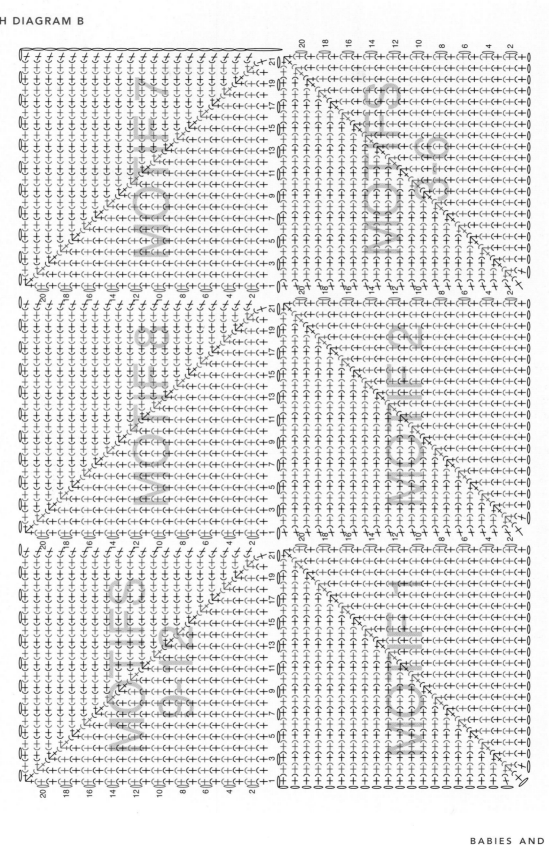

shark hunter
HAT

This hat complements the Shark Hunter Blanket on page 120. The square motifs are half the size of the blanket's squares, but ultimately follow the same pattern. Unlike other hats in this book, the crown is worked in rows of decreases for simplicity. The rigid look of the squares is maintained with the unusual seaming technique, which alternates folding right sides together and then folding wrong sides together before seaming with slip stitches.

YARN

Worsted weight (#4 Medium).

shown: Caron, Simply Soft (100% acrylic; 315 yd [288m]/6 oz [170 g]): 1 ball of # 9711 dark country blue.

HOOK

H/8 (5 mm) or size needed to obtain gauge.

NOTIONS

Tapestry needle for weaving in ends.

GAUGE

1 motif = 2¾" (7 cm) unstretched.

FINISHED SIZE

16½" (42 cm) circumference, unstretched.

Shark Hunter Hat

Refer to Stitch Diagram B at right for assistance. Shark Hunter Motif instructions begin on page 122.

Motif 1

ROW 1: Work 21 fsc.

ROW 2: Ch 1, *sc-blo in ea of next 9 sts*, sc3tog-blo, rep from * to * once, turn—19 sts.

ROW 3: Ch 1, *sc-blo in ea of next 8 sts*, sc3tog-blo, rep from * to * once, turn—17 sts.

ROW 4: Ch 1, *sc-blo in ea of next 7 sts*, sc3tog-blo, rep from * to * once, turn—15 sts.

ROWS 5–10: Cont in est patt until 3 sts rem.

ROW 11 (LAST ROW): Ch 1, sc3tog-blo. Do not fasten off.

Motifs 2–6

ROW 1: Ch 1, work 10 sc evenly along ends of rows on previous square, fsc 11 sts, turn—21 sts.

ROWS 2–11: Rep Rows 2–11 of Motif 1.

Motif 7

ROW 1: Loosely ch 11, sc in 2nd ch from hook and in ea ch across, work 11 sc evenly along ends of rows of previous square, turn—21 sts.

ROWS 2–11: Rep Rows 2–11 of Motif 1.

Motif 8

ROW 1: Ch 1, work 10 sc evenly along ends of rows on previous square, work 11 sc evenly spaced across next square in row 1, turn—21 sts.

Motifs 9–12

Rep Motif 8.

Do not fasten off.

Crown

ROW 1: Ch 1, working along long side of Motifs 12–7, work 11 sc evenly spaced across ea motif, turn—66 sc.

ROW 2: Ch 1, [sc2tog-blo, 1 sc-blo in ea of next 4 sts] 11 times, turn—55 sts.

ROW 3: Ch 1, [sc2tog-blo, 1 sc-blo in ea of next 3 sts] 11 times, turn—44 sts.

ROW 4: Ch 1, [sc2tog-blo, 1 sc-blo in ea of next 2 sts] 11 times, turn—33 sts.

ROW 5: Ch 1, [sc2tog-blo, 1 sc-blo in next st] 11 times, turn—22 sts.

ROW 6: Ch 1, [sc2tog-blo] 11 times, turn—11 sts.

ROW 7: Ch 1, [sc2tog-blo] twice, sc3tog-blo, [sc2tog-blo] twice, turn—5 sts.

ROW 8: Ch 1, sc5tog-blo—1 st.

Assembly

Note: Due to the highly textured nature of this fabric, if you alternate the side of the seam every other motif, the seam disappears.

Holding right sides facing, sl st through both thicknesses of the sides of the 7 rows of the crown (7 sl sts), fold the fabric so the wrong sides are facing and sl st through both thicknesses of the sides of Motifs 7 and 12 (11 sl sts), fold the fabric so the right sides are facing and sl st through both thicknesses of the sides of Motifs 1 and 6 (11 sl sts). Fasten off. Weave in ends.

STITCH DIAGRAM B

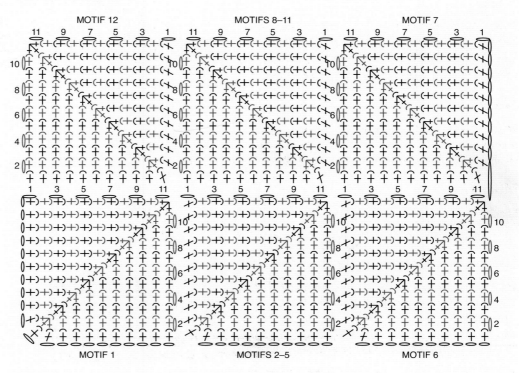

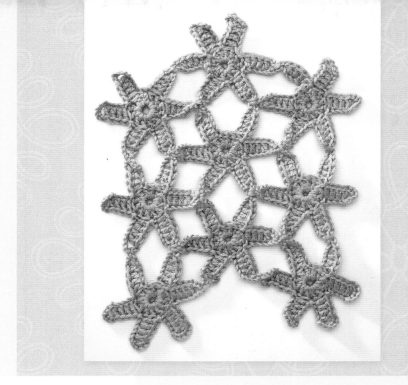

starfish
BLANKET

The star-shaped motif featured in this blanket has an unusual construction that is quite simple to master. Instead of working row after row of the same number of motifs, this blanket begins with one motif in the first row, increasing by one motif per row until the desired width is achieved, then decreasing by one motif per row for the second half of the blanket. The wide-scallop edging is then worked in rows sideways from the edge of the blanket. The finished result is a uniquely shaped throw, with a fun aquatic theme, that is ideal for brightening up a child's bedroom.

YARN

Worsted weight (#4 Medium).

shown: Lion Brand, Pound of Love (100% premium acrylic; 1020 yd [932 m]/16 oz [448 g]): 2 balls of #156 pastel green.

HOOK

K/10.5 (6.5 mm) or size needed to obtain gauge.

NOTIONS

Tapestry needle for weaving in ends.

GAUGE

With 2 strands held together, 12 sts and 6 rows dc = 4" (10 cm); 1 starfish motif = 5" (12.5 cm) in diameter.

FINISHED SIZE

46" wide x 71" long (117 x 180 cm).

starfish *motif*

STITCH DIAGRAM A

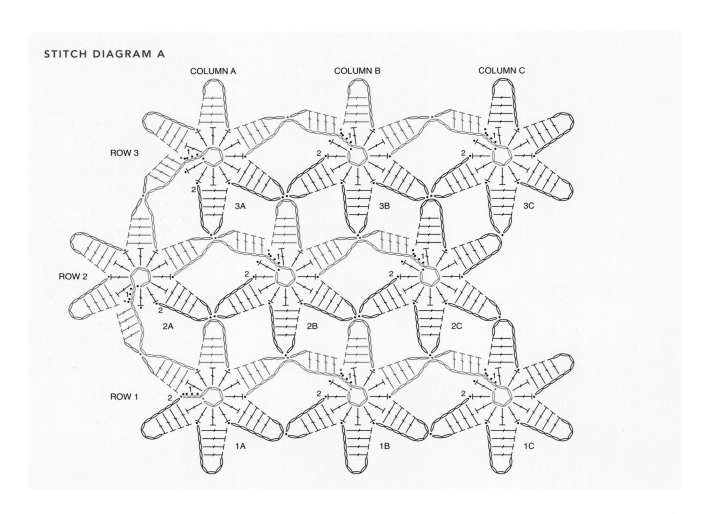

Refer to Stitch Diagram A above for assistance.

Motif 1A

RND 1: Ch 5 + 3 = 8, sl st in 5th ch from hook to join ring. Sl st in ea of next 3 chs (counts as dc), 11 dc in ring. Sl st to top of ch-3 at beg of rnd to join.

RND 2: *Ch 9, dc in 6th ch from hook, dc in ea of next 3 chs, sk next dc in Rnd 1, sl st in next dc. Rep from * twice.

Motif 1B

RND 1: Ch 5 + 3 + 4 + 9 = 21, sl st in 5th ch from hook to form ring, sl st in ea of next 3 chs (counts as dc), 11 dc in ring. Sl st to top of ch-3 at beg of rnd to join.

RND 2: Sl st in ea of next 2 dc, ch 6, sl st in ch-5 sp on adjacent motif, ch 2, sk last 4 chs made, dc in ea of next 4 chs, sk next dc in Rnd 1, sl st in next dc. *Ch 9, dc in 6th ch from hook, dc in ea of next 3 chs, sk next dc in Rnd 1, sl st in next dc. Rep from * once.

Motif 1C

RND 1: Rep Rnd 1 of Motif 1B.

RND 2: Sl st in ea of next 2 dc, ch 6, sl st in ch-5 sp on adjacent motif, ch 2, sk last 4 chs made, dc in ea of next 4 chs, sk next dc, sl st in next dc. *Ch 9, dc in 6th ch from hook, dc in ea of next 3 chs, sk next st in Rnd 1, sl st in next st. Rep from * 3 times.

Working across incomplete motifs in row 1, *dc in ea of next 4 beg chs, ch 2, sk next 2 chs, sl st in next ch, ch 2, sk next 2 ch, dc in ea of next 4 chs, sk next dc on next motif, sl st in next dc. Ch 9, dc in 6th ch from hook, dc in ea of next 4 chs, sk next dc on Rnd 1, sl st in next dc. Rep from * once.

Motif 2A

RND 1: Rep Rnd 1 of Motif 1B.

RND 2: Sl st in ea of next 2 dc, *ch 6, sl st in ch-5 sp on adjacent motif, ch 2, sk last 4 chs made, dc in ea of next 4 chs, sk next dc in Rnd 1, sl st in next dc.

Motif 2B

RND 1: Rep Rnd 1 of Motif 1B.

RND 2: Sl st in ea of next 2 dc, *ch 6, sl st in ch-5 sp on adjacent motif, ch 2, sk last 4 chs made, dc in ea of next 4 chs, sk next dc in Rnd 1, sl st in next dc. Rep from * twice.

Motif 2C

RND 1: Rep Rnd 1 of Motif 1B.

RND 2: Sl st in ea of next 2 dc, *ch 6, sl st in ch-5 sp on adjacent motif, ch 2, sk last 4 chs made, dc in ea of next 4 chs, sk next dc, sl st in next dc. Rep from * twice. **Ch 9, dc in 6th ch from hook, dc in ea of next 3 chs, sk next st in Rnd 1, sl st in next dc. Rep from ** once.

Working across incomplete motifs in row 2, dc in ea of next 4 beg chs, ch 2, sk next 2 ch, sl st in next ch, ch 2, sk next 2 ch, dc in ea of next 4 ch, sk next dc on next motif, sl st in next dc. Ch 9, dc in 6th ch from hook, dc in ea of next 3 chs, sk next dc in Rnd 1, sl st in next dc, dc in ea of next 4 beg chs, ch 2, sk next 2 ch, sl st in next ch, ch 2, sk next 2 ch, dc in ea of next 4 ch, sk next dc on next motif, sl st in next dc.

Motif 3A

RND 1: Rep Rnd 1 of Motif 1B.

RND 2: Sl st in ea of next 2 dc, *ch 6, sl st in ch-5 sp on adjacent motif, ch 2, sk last 4 chs made, dc in ea of next 4 chs, sk next dc in Rnd 1, sl st in next dc. Rep from * once.

Motif 3B

Rep Motif 2B.

Motif 3C

RND 1: Rep Rnd 1 of Motif 1B.

RND 2: Sl st in ea of next 2 dc, *ch 6, sl st in ch-5 sp on adjacent motif, ch 2, sk last 4 chs made, dc in ea of next 4 chs, sk next dc in Rnd 1, sl st in next dc. Rep from * once. **Ch 9, dc in 6th ch from hook, dc in ea of next 3 chs, sk next dc in Rnd 1, sl st in next dc. Rep from ** twice.

Working across incomplete motifs of row 3, *dc in ea of next 4 beg chs, ch 2, sk next 2 ch, sl st in next ch, ch 2, sk next 2 ch, dc in ea of next 4 ch, sk next dc on next motif, sl st in next dc. Ch 9, dc in 6th ch from hook, dc in ea of next 3 chs, sk next dc in Rnd 1, sl st in next dc. Rep from * once. Ch 9, dc in 6th ch from hook, dc in ea of next 3 chs, sk next st on Rnd 1, sl st in next st.

Working along side edge of incomplete motifs in column A, dc in ea of next 4 beg chs, ch 2, sk next 2 ch, sl st in next ch, ch 2, sk next 2 ch, dc in ea of next 4 ch, sk next dc on next motif, sl st in next dc. [Ch 9, dc in 6th ch from hook, dc in ea of next 4 chs, sk next dc in Rnd 1, sl st in next dc] twice, dc in ea of next 4 beg chs, ch 2, sk next 2 ch, sl st in next ch, ch 2, sk next 2 ch, dc in ea of next 4 ch, sk next dc on next motif, sl st in next dc. Fasten off.

Starfish Blanket

Refer to Stitch Diagram B at right and the Construction Diagram on page 136 for assistance. Starfish Motif instructions begin on page 132.

Motif 1

RND 1: Ch 5 + 3 = 8, sl st in 5th ch from hook to join ring. Sl st in ea of next 3 chs (counts as dc), 11 dc in ring. Sl st to top of ch-3 at beg of rnd to join.

RND 2: *Ch 9, dc in 6th ch from hook, dc in ea of next 3 chs, sk next st on Rnd 1, sl st in next st. Rep from * twice—3 petals made.

Motif 2

RND 1: Ch 5 + 3 + 4 + 9 = 21, sl st in 5th ch from hook to join ring. Sl st in ea of next 3 chs (counts as dc), 11 dc in ring. Sl st to top of ch-3 at beg of rnd to join.

RND 2: Sl st in ea of next 2 dc, ch 6, sl st in ch-5 sp of adjacent motif, ch 2, sk last 4 chs made, dc in ea of next 4 chs, sk next dc in Rnd 1, sl st in next dc.

Motif 3

RND 1: Rep Rnd 1 of Motif 2.

RND 2: Sl st in ea of next 2 dc, [ch 6, sl st in ch-5 sp on adjacent flower's petal, ch 2, sk last 4 chs made, dc in ea of next 4 chs, sk next dc in Rnd 1, sl st in next dc] twice, *ch 9, dc in 6th ch from hook, dc in ea of next 3 chs, sk next dc in Rnd 1, sl st in next dc. Rep from * twice.

COMPLETION ROW 1: Working across incomplete motifs in row 2, dc in ea of next 4 beg chs, ch 2, sk next 2 chs, sl st in next ch, ch 2, sk next 2 chs, dc in ea of next 4 beg chs, sk next dc on next motif, sl st in next dc. Ch 9, dc in 6th ch from hook, dc in ea of next 3 chs, sk next dc on Rnd 1, sl st in next dc.

Motif 4

Rep Motif 2.

Motif 5

RND 1: Rep Rnd 1 of Motif 2.

RND 2: Sl st in ea of next 2 dc. [Ch 6, sl st in ch-5 sp on adjacent motif, ch 2, sk last 4 chs

Note

Work with 2 strands of yarn held together as one throughout. Blanket is made in a diamond shape, beginning with 1 motif in row 1, increasing 1 motif in each row through row 9, then decrease one motif in each row until 1 motif remains in row 17.

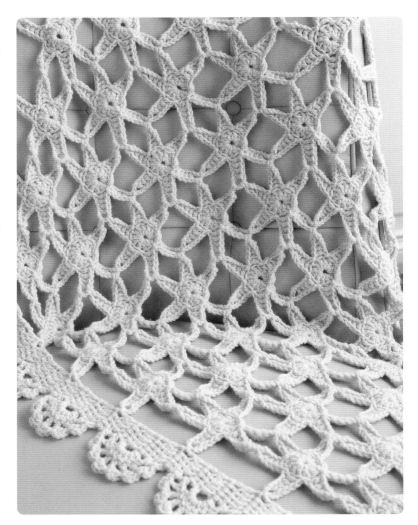

STITCH DIAGRAM B

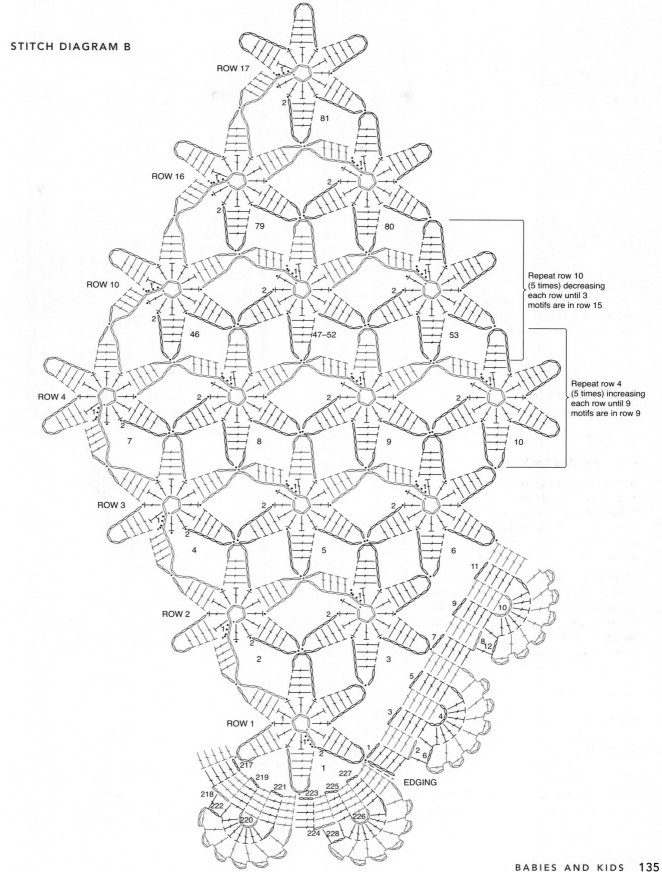

ROW 17

81

ROW 16

79

80

ROW 10

Repeat row 10
(5 times) decreasing
each row until 3
motifs are in row 15

46

47–52

53

Repeat row 4
(5 times) increasing
each row until 9
motifs are in row 9

ROW 4

7

8

9

10

ROW 3

4

5

6

11

9

10

8 12

7

5

ROW 2

2

3

3

4

2 6

ROW 1

2

1

227

1

2 6

217

219

221

223

225

EDGING

218

222

220

224 228

226

made, dc in ea of next 4 chs, sk next dc, sl st in next dc] 3 times.

Motif 6

Rep Motif 3.

COMPLETION ROW 2: Working across incomplete motifs in row 3, *dc in ea of next 4 beg chs, ch 2, sk next 2 chs, sl st in next ch, ch 2, sk next 2 chs, dc in ea of next 4 chs, sk next dc on next motif, sl st in next dc*. Ch 9, dc in 6th ch from hook, dc in ea of next 3 chs, sk next dc on Rnd 1, sl st in next dc. Rep from * to * once.

Motif 7

Rep Motif 2.

Motifs 8–9

Rep Motif 5.

Motif 10

Rep Motif 3.

COMPLETION ROW 3: Working across incomplete motifs in row, dc in ea of next 4 beg chs, ch 2, sk next 2 ch, *(sl st in next ch, ch 2, sk next 2 ch, dc in ea of next 4 chs, sk next dc on next motif, sl st in next dc*, ch 9, dc in 6th ch from hook, dc in ea of next 3 chs, sk next dc on Rnd 1, sl st in next dc, dc in ea of next 4 beg chs, ch 2, sk next 2 chs) across to last motif. Rep from * to * once.

Motif 11

Rep Motif 2.

Motifs 12–14

Rep Motif 5.

Motif 15

Rep Motif 3.
Rep Completion Row 3.

Motif 16

Rep Motif 2.

Motifs 17–20

Rep Motif 5.

CONSTRUCTION DIAGRAM

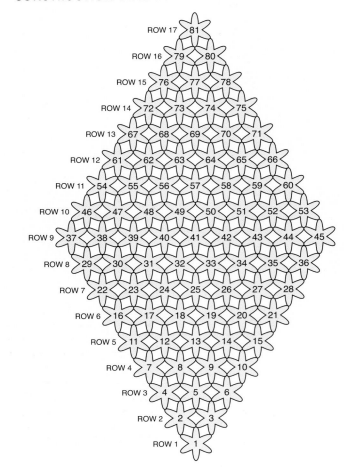

Motif 21

Rep Motif 6.
Rep Completion Row 3.

Motif 22

Rep Motif 2.

Motifs 23–27

Rep Motif 5.

Motif 28

Rep Motif 3.
Rep Completion Row 3.

Motif 29

Rep Motif 2.

Motifs 30–35

Rep Motif 5.

Motif 36

Rep Motif 3.

Rep Completion Row 3.

Motif 37

Rep Motif 2.

Motifs 38–44

Rep Motif 5.

Motif 45

Rep Motif 3.

COMPLETION ROW 4: Working across incomplete motifs in row, dc in ea of next 4 beg chs, ch 2, sk next 2 ch, (sl st in next ch, ch 2, sk next 2 ch, dc in ea of next 4 chs, sk next dc on next motif, sl st in next dc, ch 9, dc in 6th ch from hook, dc in ea of next 4 chs, sk next dc on Rnd 1, sl st in next dc, dc in ea of next 4 beg chs, ch 2, sk next 2 chs) across to last motif, sl st in next ch, ch 2, sk next 2 ch, dc in ea of next 4 chs, sk next dc on next motif, sl st in next dc.

Motif 46

RND 1: Rep Rnd 1 of Motif 2.

RND 2: Sl st in ea of next 2 dc, [ch 6, sl st in ch-5 sp of adjacent motif, ch 2, sk last 4 chs made, dc in ea of next 4 chs, sk next dc in Rnd 1, sl st in next dc] twice.

Motifs 47–52

Rep Motif 5.

Motif 53

RND 1: Rep Rnd 1 of Motif 2.

RND 2: Sl st in ea of next 2 dc, [ch 6, sl st in ch-5 sp on adjacent flower's petal, ch 2, sk last 4 chs made, dc in ea of next 4 chs, sk next dc in Rnd 1, sl st in next dc] 3 times. **Ch 9, dc in 6th ch from hook, dc in ea of next 3 chs, sk next dc in Rnd 1, sl st in next dc. Rep from ** once.

Rep Completion Row 4.

Motif 54

Rep Motif 46.

Motifs 55–59

Rep Motif 5.

Motif 60

Rep Motif 53.

Rep Completion Row 4.

Motif 61

Rep Motif 46.

Motifs 62–65

Rep Motif 5.

Motif 66

Rep Motif 53.

Rep Completion Row 4.

Motif 67

Rep Motif 46.

Motifs 68–70

Rep Motif 5.

Motif 71

Rep Motif 53.

Rep Completion Row 4.

Motif 72

Rep Motif 46.

Motifs 73–74

Rep Motif 5.

Motif 75

Rep Motif 53.

Rep Completion Row 4.

Motif 76

Rep Motif 46.

Motif 77

Rep Motif 5.

Motif 78

Rep Motif 53.

Rep Completion Row 4.

Motif 79

Rep Motif 46.

Motif 80

Rep Motif 53.

COMPLETION ROW 5: Working across incomplete motifs in row, dc in ea of next 4 beg chs, ch 2, sk next 2 chs, sl st in next ch, ch 2, sk next 2 chs, dc in ea of next 4 beg chs, sk next dc on next motif, sl st in next dc.

Motif 81

RND 1: Rep Rnd 1 of Motif 2.

RND 2: Sl st in ea of next 2 dc, [ch 6, sl st in ch-5 sp on adjacent flower's petal, ch 2, sk last 4 chs made, dc in ea of next 4 chs, sk next dc in Rnd 1, sl st in next dc] twice. *Ch 9, dc in 6th ch from hook, dc in ea of next 3 chs, sk next dc in Rnd 1, sl st in next dc. Rep from * twice.

Working across side edge of blanket, dc in ea of next 4 beg chs, ch 2, sk next 2 chs, sl st in next ch, *ch 2, sk next 2 chs, dc in ea of next 4 chs, sk next dc in Rnd 1 of next motif, sl st in next dc, ch 9, dc in 6th ch from hook, dc in ea of next 3 chs, sk next dc in Rnd 1, sl st in next st, dc in ea of next 4 beg chs, ch 2, sk next 2 chs, sl st in next ch*. Rep from * to * 6 times to complete Motifs 76, 72, 67, 61, 54, and 46. Ch 2, sk next 2 chs, dc in ea of next 4 chs, sk next dc in Rnd 1 of next motif, sl st in next dc, [ch 9, dc in 6th ch from hook, dc in ea of next 3 chs, sk next dc in Rnd 1, sl st in next st] twice, dc in

ea of next 4 beg chs, ch 2, sk next 2 chs, sl st in next ch. Rep from * to * 7 times to complete Motifs 29, 22, 16, 11, 7, 4, and 2. Ch 2, sk next 2 ch, dc in ea of next 4 beg chs, ch 2, sk next 2 chs, sl st in next dc, [ch 9, dc in 6th ch from hook, dc in ea of next 3 chs, sk next dc in Rnd 1, sl st in next st] twice, ending with last sl st in top of beg ch-3 in Motif 1. Fasten off.

Edging

Ch 4, sl st in ch-5 sp at end of first petal of Motif 1, turn.

ROW 1 (WS): Ch 3 (counts as dc here and throughout), dc in ea of next 4 ch of beg ch, turn—5 dc.

ROWS 2–3: Ch 3, sk first dc, dc in ea dc across, turn—5 dc.

ROW 4: Ch 6, dc in first dc, dc in ea dc across, turn—5 dc.

ROW 5: Ch 3, sk first dc, dc in ea dc across, ch 2, 7 dc in next ch-6 sp, dc in side of st at end of Row 3, ch 2, dc in side of st at end of Row 2, turn.

ROW 6: Ch 3, dc in 3rd ch from hook, sk next dc of 7 dcs in ch-6 sp, dc in next dc, [ch 3, dc in 3rd ch from hook, dc in next dc] 4 times, (ch 3, dc in 3rd ch from hook), sk next dc, dc in next ch-2 sp, ch 2, dc in ea of next 5 dc, sl st in ch-5 sp at tip of next petal along edge of blanket, turn.

ROW 7: Ch 3, sk first dc, dc in ea dc across—5 dc.

ROWS 8–229: Rep Rows 2–7 thirty-six times until you have worked the edging and joined it to all free petals around blanket, then work Rows 2–6 once more. Fasten off. Whipstitch last row to starting chain at beg of edging. Weave in ends.

Wet block, pin to finished measurements, and let dry.

join-as-you-go *motifs*

The Basics: Understanding the Seamless Technique

This book was designed to help you understand the exciting seamless method of crochet, using motifs to create beautiful pieces that are as enjoyable to create as they are to use.

Construction Method

The construction concept of joining-as-you-go reminds me of an old-fashioned typewriter. The typewriter would type across the page left to right, then you would hit the typewriter carriage to "return" to the left side of the page. This method of joining motifs works in a similar manner. In order to better understand this method of crocheting motifs, let's take a look at how the motifs are joined. In the Construction Diagram at right, you can see that we begin with motif 1A (in the bottom left corner). We join partial motifs in a row working left to right (row 1), then "return" across the tops of the incomplete motifs back to the left side of the row. The subsequent rows of motifs are worked left to right (while joining as you go), and the "return" across the tops of the partial motifs are completed right to left. All the while, the first motif and each motif in the first column (A) are not completed until after the last row of motifs is completed, thereby "returning" along the side edge of the first column (A) of the motifs, and finally fastening off the completed piece at the first motif (1A).

Each motif is written in this way, giving you specific line-by-line instructions for making a 3 x 3 motif square. There are unique instructions for each of these 9 motif locations: the first, middle, and last motif in the first row; the first, middle, and last motifs in the 2nd (and all

CONSTRUCTION DIAGRAM

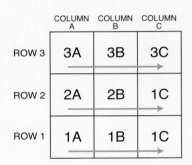

middle) row(s); and the first, middle, and last motifs in the last row. The instructions are specific to the 3 x 3 grid, because there are slight variations of "sequence of completion" for each motif location within the 3 x 3 grid. Even if your project were to be 100 motifs long or wide, the details would remain the same: 1st, 2nd–99th, and 100th. Listed below is a description of each of the 9 motif locations:

- **Motif 1A** is the first motif. It will always be written without being joined to a previous motif.

- **Motif 1B** is a middle motif in the first row of motifs. It is only joined to the previous motif (1A) on one side and partially completed on the final round. This is the motif you would repeat in row 1 for a wider fabric.

- **Motif 1C** is an end motif in the first row of motifs. It is only joined to the previous motif (1B) on one side, but it is also the beginning of the "return" of row 1. Motif 1C is completed and you continuously complete the final round of the rest of row 1 from here, ending at the top of Motif 1A.

- **Motif 2A** is the first motif on subsequent rows of motifs. It is only joined to the previous motif (1A) on one side. The outer (left) and upper sides are not completed until the "return."

- **Motif 2B** is the middle motif for the middle rows. It is joined to the previous motif (2A) on the same row and joined to the motif (1B) on the row below. It is a 2-sided join motif. This is the motif you would repeat in row 2 (and any additional middle rows) for a larger fabric.

- **Motif 2C** is an end motif in the 2nd (and any additional middle) rows. It is joined to the previous motif (2B) on the same row and joined to the motif on the row below (1C). It is a 2-sided join motif. It is also the beginning of the "return" of row 2 (and any additional middle rows). Motif 2C is completed, and you continuously complete the final round of the rest of row 2 (and any additional middle rows) from here, ending at the top of motif 2A.

- **Motif 3A** is the first motif on the final row of motifs. It is only joined to the previous motif (2A) one row below on one side. The outer left and upper sides are completed during the "return" of row 3 (or the final row of motifs).

- **Motif 3B** is the middle motif on the final row of motifs. It is joined to the previous motif (3A) on the same row of motifs and joined to the motif on the row below (2B). It is a 2-sided join motif. This is the motif you would repeat in the final row for a larger fabric.

- **Motif 3C** is the end motif in the last row of motifs. It is joined to the previous motif (3B) on the same row and joined to the motif on the row below (2C). It is a 2-sided join motif. It is also the beginning of the "return" of the 3rd (or final) row of motifs. Motif 3C is completed, and you continuously complete the final round of the rest of row 3 from here, then continuing on to complete the final round of the motifs in column A, ending with fastening off at motif 1A.

Symbol Crochet

How to Read Symbol Crochet:

Symbol diagrams are a wonderful addition to a crochet pattern because they are a visual aid that helps you discern how your project is supposed to look as you go along. Once you learn the universal crochet symbols used, you can read any crochet symbol diagram in the world, no matter what language the accompanying text is written in.

SYMBOL CROCHET KEY

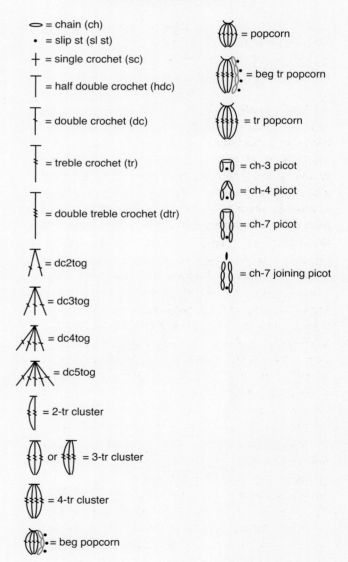

First, read the symbol key and get familiar with the crochet stitches each symbol represents. For example, a small oval is usually a chain, a short cross is a single crochet, and a slip stitch is usually represented by a small solid dot. Usually, you will find that a motif diagram begins with a starting chain, joined in a ring in the center. From there the rounds of crochet are worked in a counterclockwise direction (for right-handers; if crocheting left-handed you would work in a clockwise direction). You will also see a small number near the beginning of each round, which indicates the round you are crocheting (so 1 indicates Rnd 1, 2 indicates Rnd 2, etc. . . .).

Seamless Symbol Crochet Diagrams

You've just learned how to read a basic symbol crochet diagram. However, in order to crochet and join motifs seamlessly, you will need to be able to read the unique diagrams for seamless crochet contained in this book.

The diagrams are color-coded, and each color has a specific meaning. The long beginning chain of every motif is red. You will start from the outside edge and work toward the center, joining into the center ring. The interior rounds and the bottom portion of the exterior joining round are black. The upper portion of the joining round is blue (along the top edge of each row). The side edge portion of the joining round (along the side edge of the left column of motifs) is purple (refer to Diagrams A–J and the corresponding step-by-step instructions, beginning below, to see examples of this color coding).

In order to fully understand how these diagrams work, let's walk through the process, step by step.

First, we make a beginning chain for motif #1 that is long enough for the ring and the starting chain for each round (**Stitch Diagram A**).

STITCH DIAGRAM A

Motif 1

Ch 5 + 4 = 9, sl st in 5th ch from hook to form ring.

Next we work Rnd 1 around in a counterclockwise direction, ending with joining to the beginning chain at the correct height (**Stitch Diagram B**).

STITCH DIAGRAM B

RND 1: [Ch 4, 3-tr cluster in ring, ch 4, sl st in ring] 3 times, ch 4, 3-tr cluster in ring, sl st to 4th ch of beg ch.

Now, we begin Rnd 2. This is the joining round, so this will be worked in separate steps as you join the motifs together (**Stitch Diagram C**).

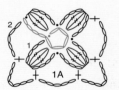

STITCH DIAGRAM C

RND 2: Ch 5, sc in next ch-4 sp, ch 7, sc in next ch-4 sp, ch 5, sc in next ch-4 sp, ch 7, sc in next ch-4 sp, ch 5, sc in next ch-4 sp. Do not fasten off.

Now, we make the starting chain for the next motif. This and all future motifs have a longer starting chain because we are adding half of the joining corner chains. You'll recognize this when we join two motifs at a corner (**Stitch Diagram D**).

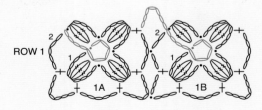

STITCH DIAGRAM D

Motif 1B

Ch 5 + 4 + 7 = 16, sl st in 5th ch from hook to form ring.

RND 1: Rep Rnd 1 of Motif 1A.

RND 2: Ch 2, sl st in ch-5 sp on adjacent motif (Motif 1A), ch 2, sc in next ch-4 sp on current motif, ch 3, sl st in 4th ch of ch-7 sp on adjacent motif (Motif 1A), ch 3, sc in next ch-4 sp on current motif, ch 5, sc in next ch-4 sp, ch 7, sc in next ch-4 sp, ch 5, sc in next ch-4 sp (**Stitch Diagram E**).

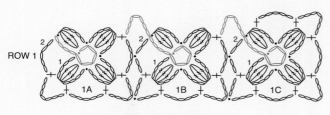

STITCH DIAGRAM E

Motif 1C

Ch 5 + 4 + 7 = 16, sl st in 5th ch from hook to form ring.

RND 1: Rep Rnd 1 of Motif 1A.

RND 2: Ch 2, sl st in ch-5 sp on adjacent motif, ch 2, sc in next ch-4 sp on current motif, ch 3, sl st in 4th ch of ch-7 sp on adjacent motif, ch 3, sc in next ch-4 sp on current motif, [ch 5, sc in next ch-4 sp, ch 7, sc in next ch-4 sp] twice, ch 5, sc in next ch-4 sp.

We've now come to the partial joining row of Row 1 of motifs (and all middle rows of motifs; **Stitch Diagram F**).

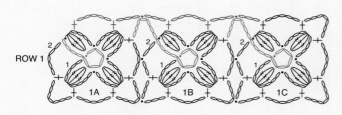

STITCH DIAGRAM F

CONTINUATION OF ROW 1 OF MOTIFS 1C, 1B, AND 1A: Working across incomplete motifs in Row 1, Ch 3, sl st in 4th ch of ch-7 of Motif 1C, ch 3, sc in next ch-4 sp of Motif 1B, ch 5, sc in next ch-4 sp of Motif 1B, ch 3, sl st in 4th ch of ch-7 of Motif 1B, ch 3, sc in next ch-4 sp of Motif 1A, ch 5, sc in next ch-4 sp of Motif 1A (**Stitch Diagram G**).

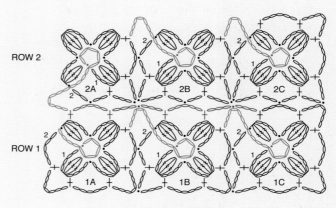

STITCH DIAGRAM G

Motif 2A

Ch 16, sl st in 5th ch from hook to form ring.

RND 1: Rep Rnd 1 of Motif 1.

RND 2: Ch 2, sl st in ch-5 sp on adjacent motif, ch 2, sc in next ch-4 sp on current motif, ch 3, sl st in 4th ch of ch-7 sp on adjacent motif, ch 3, sc in next ch-4 sp on current motif, ch 5, sc in next ch-4 sp.

Motif 2B

Ch 16, sl st in 5th ch from hook to form ring.

RND 1: Rep Rnd 1 of Motif 1A.

RND 2: [Ch 2, sl st in ch-5 sp on adjacent motif, ch 2, sc in next ch-4 sp on current motif, ch 3, sl st in 4th ch of ch-7 sp on adjacent motif, ch 3, sc in next ch-4 sp on current motif] twice, ch 5, sc in next ch-4 sp.

Motif 2C

Ch 16, sl st in 5th ch from hook to form ring.

RND 1: Rep Rnd 1 of Motif 1.

RND 2: [Ch 2, sl st in ch-5 sp on adjacent motif, ch 2, sc in next ch-4 sp on current motif, ch 3, sl st in 4th ch of ch-7 sp on adjacent motif, ch 3, sc in next ch-4 sp on current motif] twice, ch 5, sc in next ch-4 sp, ch 7, sc in next ch-4 sp, ch 5, sc in next ch-4 sp.

We've now come to the partial joining row of Row 2 (**Stitch Diagram H**).

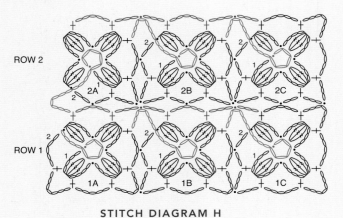

ROW 2

ROW 1

STITCH DIAGRAM H

CONTINUATION OF ROW 2 OF MOTIFS 2C, 2B, AND 2A: Ch 3, sl st in 4th ch of ch-7 of Motif 2C, ch 3, sc in next ch-4 sp of Motif 2B, ch 5, sc in next ch-4 sp of Motif 2B, ch 3, sl st in 4th ch of ch-7 of Motif 2B, ch 3, sc in next ch-4 sp of Motif 2A, ch 5, sc in next ch-4 sp of Motif 2A (**Stitch Diagram I**).

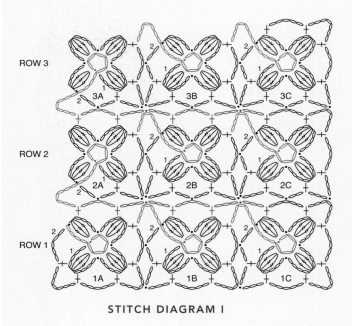

ROW 3

ROW 2

ROW 1

STITCH DIAGRAM I

ROW 3: Worked the same as Row 2.

Motif 3A:

Rep Motif 2A.

Motif 3B:

Rep Motif 2B.

Motif 3C:

Rep Motif 2C.

We've now come to the partial joining row of Row 3 of motifs (**Stitch Diagram J**).

CONTINUATION OF ROW 3 OF MOTIFS 3C, 3B, AND 3A: Ch 3, sl st in 4th ch of ch-7 of Motif 3C, ch 3, sc in next ch-4 sp of Motif 3B, ch 5, sc in next ch-4 sp of Motif 3B, ch 3, sl st in 4th ch of ch-7 of Motif 3B, ch 3, sc in next ch-4 sp of Motif 3A, ch 5, sc in next ch-4 sp of Motif 3A, ch 7, sc in next ch-4 sp on Motif 3A, ch 5, sc in next ch-4 sp on Motif 3A.

Finally, we will continue working across the side edge of column A, until all outside edges are completed (**Stitch Diagram J**).

Ch 3, sl st in 4th ch of next ch-7 in Motif 3A, ch 3, sc in next ch-4 sp in Motif 2A, ch 5, sc in next ch-4 sp in Motif 2A, ch 3, sl st in 4th ch of ch-7 sp in Motif 2A, ch 3, sl st in first ch of next ch-5 sp in Motif 1A to join. Fasten off. Enjoy weaving in only two tails for the whole project!!

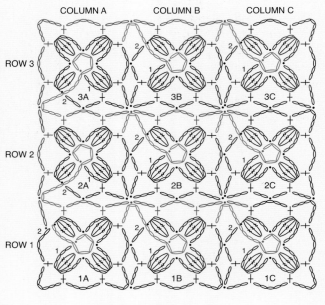

COLUMN A   COLUMN B   COLUMN C

ROW 3

ROW 2

ROW 1

STITCH DIAGRAM J

Beyond the Basics:
Tips and Techniques for Seamless Crochet

Now that you understand how the seamless crochet diagrams work, here is some information about working with motifs that goes a little beyond the basics.

Modifications to Motifs

There are several simple methods for modifying motifs to achieve a different look and fabric texture.

Changing the joining location of the Motifs

A 4-sided motif (square) can be joined along all four sides for a "tiled" fabric, or you can join them at the points for a diamond-patterned fabric. An 8-sided motif can be joined with 2 motifs per each of the 4 sides, or it can be joined with 4 sides and 4 central corners.

Changing the shape of a Motif

To change the shape, increase the beginning chain (to form the starting ring) by 1 chain for each additional repeat desired. For example, if you want to change a square that has a ch-5 starting ring to a hexagon, you would start by increasing the beginning chain by 2 chains to form a ch-7 starting ring. Then when you work Rnd 1, work the repeat 6 times instead of 4 times, to form a hexagon instead of a square.

In addition to the suggestions above, the hats included in this book are an exploration of how to manipulate the motifs for shaping purposes. The hats are made using squares around the sides to form a tube. The design of the square motif is then altered to the shape of a triangle by working 3 repeats instead of 4. The triangle motifs are arranged around the top of the tube to form the crown.

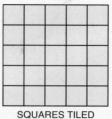

SQUARES TILED
(LINEAR JOINS)

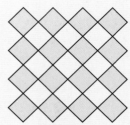

SQUARES USED
AS DIAMONDS
(JOINED AT CORNERS ONLY)

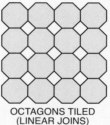

OCTAGONS TILED
(LINEAR JOINS)

OCTAGONS
JOINED AT ONE POINT
(JOINED AT CORNERS ONLY)

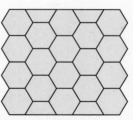

HEXAGONS TILED
(LINEAR JOINS)

HEXAGONS JOINED
AT CORNERS ONLY

Joining Motifs to Form a Tube

The seamless method of crocheting explained earlier can easily be modified for forming a tube (for example, the Jamie Hat on page 84 and the Lace Flower Hat on page 58); the concept is quite simple and can be applied to any motif fabric. Your fabric, however large or small, is worked flat until the last joining round. When you complete the top of the last row of motifs and turn to complete the remaining round of motifs in column A, you need to join these motifs to the finished edge of the motifs in column C (or the opposite side edge of the motif fabric).

Note: If you are joining the fabric for a tube, make sure you don't twist the fabric when joining.

Modifying Motifs for Tail-Free Construction

This book contains a library of beautiful motifs ready to crochet seamlessly. However, many traditional motifs can be converted into the seamless technique with a little forethought. Simply put, you need to crochet the beginning chain of each round as one long chain before beginning the motif. For example, let's say your motif has a ch-5, joined in a ring to begin, and ch 3 at the beginning of each of 3 double crochet rounds; you will need to ch 5 + 3 + 3 + 3 = 14 for your starting chain. After the initial joining to form a ring, as you begin each round, sl st up the long chain for the required number of chs in your beg of round chain (3 ch for each round to achieve the height of the double crochet). At the end of the round, sl st to the top of the ch-3 that counts as the double crochet, as usual.

Combining Motifs in the Tail-Free Technique

Any motif shape can be joined together in a variety of ways, and depending on how much negative space you want in your fabric design, you have many choices.

Making a fabric using a variety of motifs (rather than a single motif) in the seamless technique is another alternative to consider. First, you will need to make sure the motifs are similar in size and shape so the sides will line up when joining. You will also need to consider where and how often you are going to join them together. For instance, they might be joined in just one corner or several times across each side. Planning your arrangement requires a little forethought, but the geometric design elements of your finished fabric will be worth the effort!

Glossary

Abbreviations

beg	beginning
bet	between
blo	through back loop(s) only
bp	back post
ch	chain
ch-(sp)	chain (or space) previously made
cl	cluster
cm	centimeter(s)
cont	continue(s), continuing
dc	double crochet
dtr	double treble crochet
ea	each
est	established
fp	front post
fsc	foundation single crochet
g	gram(s)
hdc	half double crochet
m	meter(s)
patt	pattern(s)
rem	remain(s); remaining
rnd	round
rep	repeat; repeating
RS	right side(s)
RSC	reverse single crochet
sc	single crochet
sk	skip
sl st	slip stitch
sp	space(s)
st(s)	stitch(s)
tog	together
tr	treble crochet
WS	wrong side(s)
yd	yard(s)
yo	yarn over
*	repeat instructions following asterisk as directed
**	repeat all instructions between asterisks as directed
()	alternate instructions and/or measurements
[]	work bracketed instructions specified number of times

Gauge

The quickest way to check gauge is to make a square of fabric about 4" (10 cm) wide by 4" (10 cm) tall (or motif indicated in pattern for gauge) with the suggested hook size and in the indicated stitch. If your measurements match the measurements of the pattern's gauge, congratulations! If you have too many stitches, try going up a hook size, if you have too few stitches, try going down a hook size. Crochet another swatch with the new hook until your gauge matches what is indicated in the pattern.

If the gauge has been measured after blocking, be sure to wet your swatch and block it before taking measurements to check gauge. Wet blocking drastically affects the gauge measurement, especially in lace stitch work.

Blocking

Blocking allows the fabric to relax and ensures proper shape, measurements, and drape of the fabric. After time and wear, you will still want to block your garment after washings to bring it back to its original shape. Remember to treat wool fibers carefully when wetting or washing to block. Avoid felting by staying away from hot water and agitation (from a washing machine or water removal by hand). Also remember to keep synthetic fibers (e.g., acrylic) away from high heat.

Blocking can be achieved by wet blocking or steam blocking. Wet blocking involves pinning a wet piece to finished measurements and allowing the piece to air-dry. Steam blocking is achieved by pinning the piece to finished measurements (dry) and then using a steamer or steam iron to gently steam the entire piece (do not touch the iron directly to the fabric), and then allowing the piece to air-dry.

Crochet Stitches and Techniques

Chain Stitch (ch)

Make a slipknot on hook. *Yo and draw through loop on hook. Repeat from *.

Single Crochet (sc)

*Insert hook in next st, yo and draw up a loop (Figure 1), yo and draw through both loops on hook (Figure 2). Repeat from *.

FIGURE 1   FIGURE 2

Slip Stitch (sl st)

*Insert hook in next st, yo and draw loop through stitch and loop on hook. Repeat from *.

Half Double Crochet (hdc)

*Yo, insert hook in next st, yo and draw up a loop (3 loops on hook), yo (Figure 1) and draw through all the loops on the hook (Figure 2). Repeat from *.

FIGURE 1   FIGURE 2

Double Crochet (dc)

*Yo, insert hook into a st, yo and draw up a loop (3 loops on hook; Figure 1), yo and draw through 2 loops (Figure 2), yo and draw through 2 loops, yarn over hook and draw it through the rem 2 loops (Figure 3). Repeat from *.

FIGURE 1

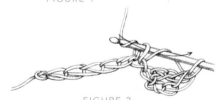

FIGURE 2

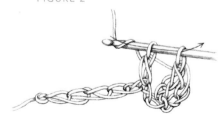

FIGURE 3

Double Crochet 2 Together (dc2tog)

[Yo, insert hook in next st, yo and draw up a loop, yo and draw through 2 loops] twice (3 loops on hook). Yo, pull though all remaining loops on hook—1 decrease made.

Double-Treble Crochet (dtr)

*Yo (3 times), insert hook into a st, yo and draw up a loop (5 loops on hook). [Yarn over hook and draw it through 2 loops] 4 times. Repeat from *.

Treble Crochet (tr)

*Yo twice, insert hook in next st, yo and draw up a loop (4 loops on hook; Figure 1), yo and draw it through 2 loops (Figure 2), yo and draw it through the remaining 2 loops (Figure 3). Repeat from *.

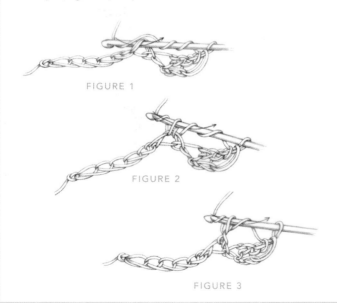

FIGURE 1

FIGURE 2

FIGURE 3

Whipstitch

With right sides of work facing and working through edge stitch(es), bring threaded needle out from back to front, along edge of piece.

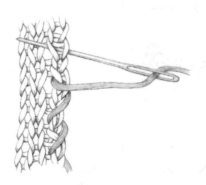

Resources

THE ALPACA YARN
COMPANY

(866) 440-7222

144 Roosevelt Ave. Bay #1

York, PA 17401

thealpacayarnco.com

Glimmer

BIJOU BASIN RANCH

(303) 601-7544

PO Box 154

Elbert, CO 80106

bijoubasinranch.com

Bijou Bliss

CARON INTERNATIONAL

Customer Service

PO Box 222

Washington, NC 27889

caron.com

Naturally Caron, Spa; Simply Soft

COATS & CLARK

(800) 648-1479

Consumers Services

PO Box 12229

Greenville, SC 29612-0229

coatsandclark.com

Eco-Ways; Red Heart
Econo Super Saver

LION BRAND YARN

(800) 258-9276

135 Kero Rd.

Carlstadt, NJ 07072

lionbrand.com

Lion Cotton; Hometown USA

LORNA'S LACES

(773) 935-3803

4229 N. Honore St.

Chicago, IL 60613

lornaslaces.net

Honor

LOUET NORTH AMERICA

(800) 897-6444

3425 Hands Rd.

Prescott, ON

Canada KDE 1TO

louet.com

Euroflax Linen Sportweight

MALABRIGO YARN

(786) 866-6187

malabrigoyarn.com

Rios

TAHKI STACY CHARLES

(800) 337-9276

70-30 80th St., Bldg. 36

Ridgewood, NY 11385

tahkistacycharles.com

Tivoli

TILLI TOMAS

(617) 524-3330

tillitomas.com

Symphony Lace; Plie

Index

r more
crochet

se popular crochet
resources from Interweave

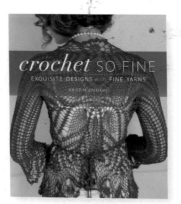

Crochet So Fine
Exquisite Designs
with Fine Yarns

Kristin Omdahl

ISBN 978-1-59668-198-9
$22.95

Wrapped In Crochet
Scarves, Wraps & Shawls

Kristin Omdahl

ISBN 978-1-59668-076-0
$22.95

The Best of
Interweave Crochet
A Collection of Our
Favorite Designs

Marcy Smith

ISBN 978-1-59668-302-0
$24.95

fueling the crochet revolution

Want to CrochetMe?

Crochet Me is an online community
that shares your passion for all things
crochet. Browse through our free
patterns, read our blogs, check our
galleries, chat in the forums, make a
few friends. Sign up at **crochetme.com**

INTERWEAVE
CROCHET

From cover to cover, *Interw*
magazine presents great
the beginner to the ad
Every issue is packed
smart designs, ste
easy-to-understa
well-written, liv
interweavecr

Index

Want more designer crochet patterns?

Check out these popular crochet resources from Interweave

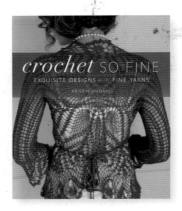

Crochet So Fine
Exquisite Designs with Fine Yarns

Kristin Omdahl
ISBN 978-1-59668-198-9
$22.95

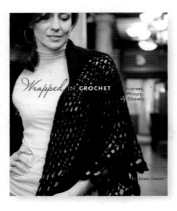

Wrapped In Crochet
Scarves, Wraps & Shawls

Kristin Omdahl
ISBN 978-1-59668-076-0
$22.95

The Best of Interweave Crochet
A Collection of Our Favorite Designs

Marcy Smith
ISBN 978-1-59668-302-0
$24.95

crochetme
fueling the crochet revolution

Want to CrochetMe?

Crochet Me is an online community that shares your passion for all things crochet. Browse through our free patterns, read our blogs, check our galleries, chat in the forums, make a few friends. Sign up at **crochetme.com**

INTERWEAVE CROCHET

From cover to cover, *Interweave Crochet* magazine presents great projects for the beginner to the advanced crocheter. Every issue is packed full of captivating smart designs, step-by-step instructions, easy-to-understand illustrations, plus well-written, lively articles sure to inspire. **interweavecrochet.com**

crochetme shop
shop.crochetme.com